MEETING DESIGN

For Managers, Makers, and Everyone

KEVIN M. HOFFMAN

TWO WAVES
BOOKS

TWO WAVES BOOKS
BROOKLYN, NY, USA

S0-DQV-668

Meeting Design
For Managers, Makers, and Everyone
By Kevin M. Hoffman

Two Waves Books
an Imprint of Rosenfeld Media, LLC
540 President Street
Brooklyn, New York
11215 USA

On the Web: twowavesbooks.com
Please send errors to: errata@twowavesbooks.com

Publisher: Louis Rosenfeld
Managing Editor: Marta Justak
Illustrations: Matt Sutter
Interior Layout Tech: Danielle Foster
Cover and Interior Design: The Heads of State
Indexer: Marilyn Augst
Proofreader: Sue Boshers

ISBN: 1-933820-38-1
ISBN 13: 978-1-933820-38-5
LCCN: 2017934295

Printed and bound in the United States of America

Kevin:
Marta suggested that I should
dedicate my book to you.

Angela:
You should write
"Thank you for not divorcing me
during the writing of this book."

Kevin:
That's funny, but what if
something happens to us down the road?
That's like having a tattoo of an ex's name.
Been there, done that.

Angela:
True.

Contents at a Glance

Contents and Executive Summary

Meetings aren't doing the work they should be doing.

Frame, build, optimize, facilitate, and measure meetings that do a job.

Think like a designer about the gatherings already taking place.

Design conversations to work effectively within limits posed by the human brain.

How much content can be covered? How many people can you invite? How much time will this agenda take?

Build from a classic definition of facilitation that works in any organization, and find productive conflict that moves things forward.

Sometimes, great facilitation can be as simple as asking the right question. But other times, a facilitator may need to adapt.

Foreword

When I was commuting regularly to New York City for work, I'd look at my calendar on the train ride in and see what meetings lay ahead. Based on how productive I felt each one was going to be, I'd plan out how to pass the time in the meeting. For most, I figured I could knock out some email on my phone under the table. For a couple, I could probably get away with answering some questions from my team in chat. For one, two max, I knew I'd have to pay attention and participate and, in all likelihood, show up prepared.

Why? What was the difference between these meetings where I knew I could tune out versus the ones where I'd have to lean in?

Let's face it—most of my meetings were awful. They were hastily called, poorly planned, and involved far too many people to yield any kind of traction. So what's the solution? It seems to be more meetings. When you add in every company's adoption of Agile rituals—stand-ups, iteration planning meetings, and retrospectives—and multiply that times the number of projects each person supports, it becomes a miracle that anything actually ever gets done at work.

And yet, to do our best work, collaboration is required. It's a successful company's secret weapon. We need to meet with our colleagues, hear their opinions, debate options, and make clear the decisions on the next steps.

But how many meetings have you attended recently that actually yielded concrete next steps and felt like a good use of your time? If you're like most people, the answer is probably pretty low. Creating great meetings is a people problem. It requires empathy for the participants, as well as a clear sense of their goals and the decision-making framework for not only deciding how to structure the meeting but whether one should happen at all.

In the software world, we advocate for changing our mindset from one focused on outputs—delivering features—to one motivated to drive outcomes—meaningful and measurable changes in customer behaviors. This mindset reshapes our definition of "done." The same model can be applied to meetings. In some organizations, the measure of success for some people is how many meetings they attend (i.e., output). The goal is, seemingly, to spend as much time in meetings to showcase the individual's productivity, importance, and contributions. How do we know that this contribution yielded anything positive to the cause we're pursuing? Just because the meetings took place doesn't mean that we had an impact of any kind on the success of our team, project, or company.

Instead, how can we figure out what outcomes our colleagues are trying to achieve by attending this meeting? Our job should be to design solutions that help them reach those outcomes. Sometimes that will be a meeting. In other cases, it might be some other activity or no activity at all.

In *Meeting Design*, Kevin lays out exactly how to take on meetings as a design problem, but you don't have to be a designer to appreciate this advice. He deftly illustrates how the designer's toolkit—a collection of questions, activities, and conversations—can be applied to create the best outcomes for these age-old activities.

Kevin applies design thinking in tactical ways to teach you how to learn what your colleagues truly need. His approach lays out tactic after tactic for structuring agendas, ensuring broad, active participation, and guaranteeing that no one leaves another meeting again feeling that time was wasted. Perhaps most importantly, he provides a clear way to assess whether a meeting is actually required and how to push back to sharpen its focus or cancel it altogether.

I've had the pleasure of spending time with Kevin personally and professionally. I've always been impressed by his balance of detailed research, pragmatism, and sense of humor, which all translate to a remarkably well-thought-out and useful book.

—Jeff Gothelf, designer, Agile practitioner, and author of
Sense and Respond: How Successful Organizations Listen to Customers and Create New Products Continuously and
Lean UX: Designing Great Products with Agile Teams

Introduction

Meetings Are a Design Problem

How well do the meetings you have every day do their intended job?

Before you answer, consider how much of your career is spent in meetings. In more than twenty years of working in design, I've been in thousands of them. Some were good, but many weren't—filled with agendaless rambling, unstructured discussion without outcomes, and needless aversion to conflict. And I'm the first to admit that I've made many meeting mistakes along the way. I've doodled out of boredom, distracted myself with unrelated emails and text messages, and even fallen asleep at least once—OK, maybe twice.

These negative experiences happened during a time when meetings were supposedly getting better. You can find new approaches to meetings in business and management books, workshop design and sketch facilitation books, online meeting software, agile approaches to software development, and dozens of blogs, websites, and magazines. Despite these new approaches, most people still find that they have more meetings than they like, and those meetings aren't any better than they used to be. If you're a manager or you run a company, that quantity-to-quality ratio is worse: you might feel as though meetings are all that you do.

Meetings *should* add value to your life by providing a sense of progress—problems being defined, decisions getting made, priorities being prioritized, and solutions being built upon the benefit of multiple perspectives. But meetings become a lazy reflex. You show up for as many meetings on your calendar as you can, but don't feel fully present in all of them. When you question that reflex, it will help you have meetings that do a better job of working *for* you.

Why Do I Care About Meetings?

When I first joined the workforce, I was unprepared for how much of my work would be dependent upon the success or failure within meetings. As part of my first full-time job working in the public library system of Baltimore, Maryland, I attended community group meetings where neighborhood residents tried to build consensus on what changes could improve their lives and the lives of their families. But conflicting community values—such as strong emotions about a neighborhood competing with strong respect for different viewpoints within a neighborhood—resulted in meandering, unproductive conversations. Discussions were democratic to a fault. Everyone contributed, but it seemed never-ending and full of irrelevant tangents. Strong personalities ruled the day while quiet people with good ideas went unheard. It was as fascinating to me as it was frustrating.

That mix of fascination and frustration with meetings followed me throughout my career of leading and facilitating large digital design projects for design agencies, as well as my own design consultancy. My clients put tremendous thought and energy into developing a project's scope before fighting for the dollars, people, and partnerships to turn that scope into a reality. But too often I've seen projects littered with thoughtless meetings, devoid of any progress-fueling energy whatsoever. Here's a classic example: an hour spent listening to a client read requirements aloud over the phone. A better use of that time would be to read those documents beforehand and use the meeting to understand—or even begin to solve—the problems we were facing (see Figure I.1).

FIGURE I.1 The dreaded document review, when you assemble . . . to just read.

After one aimless discussion, I decided that the meetings themselves could be reframed as a design problem. This simple premise—a meeting is something that could be designed to be useful and compelling—opens up a world of possibilities. You can understand more about why meetings fail by getting to know their design constraints. You can observe relationships between facilitation style, organizational culture, and the outcomes the meeting should produce. By taking a design approach to meetings, it's possible to improve their effectiveness, even within big, complex businesses. It requires applying the same level of research and intention as you would to other design process targets, such as a website or a brand.

I Want to Help You Do Your Job in Meetings

I'll bet you've had similar negative experiences with meetings in your career. This book provides a foundation to design your approach to meetings in two parts. Part 1, "The Theory and Practice of Meeting Design," begins with a simple method to measure how well your meetings are doing their intended job. Then it lists meeting design constraints, presents an agenda design approach, explores facilitation methods, and provides helpful patterns that should improve the job any meeting is doing for you. Part 2, "Designed Meetings," includes templates for common meeting types with sample agendas that you can and should extend and customize for your needs.

If having bad meetings is a problem where you are employed, these approaches can make your job, and the work of your colleagues and collaborators, easier. When people in an organization become familiar with better-designed meetings, the organization itself matures. Everyone on the team becomes more aware of a company's meeting habits and develops the kind of flexibility that keeps gatherings effective.

The title of this book refers to two kinds of people: makers and managers. Everyone falls somewhere between these two identities. These correlate with the natural evolution of any career. You start your career as a maker by making things, such as software, documents, code, or other products and outcomes. The more success you have, the more likely you are to take on the responsibility of overseeing other people who make the things you used to make, and you become a manager.

If you are a maker, you can use the checklist presented in Chapter 1, "How to Design a Meeting," to take a critical look at the meetings you get pulled into. In the following chapters, there are ways for you to improve meetings even when you aren't in charge, with hacks for the ones that aren't working and patterns to accelerate the ones that are. Both the checklist and the techniques that follow will help you make more stuff (ideas, decisions, even software) within your meetings and spend less time in meetings that aren't helping you make anything useful.

When you begin leading meetings, you have a responsibility to model behaviors that will result in positive outcomes—those decisions, priorities, and solutions mentioned earlier. But with the responsibility of management comes the power to call meetings, and it's a power that's easy to abuse. This book will help you establish good reasons for calling your meeting, as well as behavioral boundaries that will build trust and help you tailor your meetings to fit the company's cultural constraints. It will also help you be a better manager by leading meetings that empower your team to find more interesting solutions to tough problems.

I've interviewed a number of my colleagues about how they have been more intentional with their meetings, what's been successful for them, and why. A few of them were nice enough to contribute a sidebar. I've peppered their unique insights throughout the book. Hopefully their mix of easy-to-apply ideas and considered analysis will help you as much as it has helped me.

I wrote this book for one simple reason: like it or not, meetings are a part of your job, no matter what you do. My goal is to help you be better at your job by having better meetings.

1

The Theory and Practice of Meeting Design

Meetings can create great outcomes if you want them to: new ideas, better strategies, stronger relationships, good decisions, and organizational changes. These outcomes come from being intentional with the time you spend together. Meeting design is the practice of expressing that intention.

Anyone can learn and practice this skill, regardless of your experience, position, seniority, or type of workplace. Once established, a good process of meeting design will help you construct effective agendas that address how people think, how to follow time constraints, and even what could be the bad habits of your organization. With practice, you'll be able to manage conflict more effectively, define your own facilitation style, and change your style to suit the job at hand. Intentionally conceived meetings will become a window into better relationships with your work and the people you do that work with.

1

How to Design
a Meeting

When hundreds of hours of his design team's sweat, blood, and tears seemed to go up in flames in a single meeting with a group of vice presidents, Jim could have easily panicked. So that's what he did.

Jim is a creative director at a successful and highly respected boutique design agency—let's call it "Rocket Design." He found a fantastic opportunity for Rocket through a former coworker's new job at a Fortune 100 client—they were ready to spend half a million dollars to build the best website experience possible in a competitive market: online meal delivery. After several weeks of discovery, his team had assembled a design direction that they believed could be effective. Baked into a collection of mocked-up mobile screens were strategies guiding content voice, brand execution, photographic style, and user interface functionality. To move into the next phase, Jim's job was to make sure that the senior leadership at the company believed in the proposed direction just as strongly as his team did. Project managers on the client side navigated the rat's nest of the leadership's meeting availability to find a standing monthly hour in which Jim and his team could provide progress updates.

At one of these check-in meetings, Jim walked the gathered group of vice presidents and directors through a series of screens, stopping to accent unique elements and key decisions along the way. Despite asking people to hold questions until the end, there were a handful of odd interruptions, like this gem:

"That's a really strong yellow. I just don't know about that."

Jim found the interruptions unnerving, each one forcing him to reset his presentation rhythm and remind the group to wait until he was finished. When he reached the end of his walkthrough, a bit rattled, he opened the floor for an unstructured session of comments and questions. The comments and questions came fast, furious, and, of course, unstructured, like invaders from all sides breaching a fortified position:

"What will you do differently to accommodate our unique business rules around delivery partners?"

"This must work within our existing JavaScript framework, so that will happen, right?"

"Were you aware that we've got an internal team working on this exact same issue, and they've already wireframed the whole thing?"

Jim struggled through, answering each off-topic comment and occasionally handing questions off to the most qualified individuals on his team. But his frustration wasn't masked in the slightest: Jim interrupted people mid-comment, stammered when surprised, and answered brusquely with "that's out of scope!" in response to the last few questions.

In conceiving the agenda for this presentation, Jim made an error that nearly cost his team the project. He didn't design the conversation to help key stakeholders understand what had gone into all of these decisions. Instead, he did what he had learned to do by example from his boss, the previous creative director, which is often how agencies teach people to present work. Jim provided a "real estate tour" of the finished product, assuming the rationale behind the designs was obvious. But to client leadership that hadn't been along for the ride, the destination was startling and unclear.

What Is a Well-Designed Meeting?

Well-designed things make our lives simpler or more pleasing. *Design* is an intangible currency that separates things that matter from junk. Something designed has been given appropriate and actionable consideration, with forethought and research guiding its creation and ongoing evolution.

Meetings are usually *not* designed. They are rather used as blunt force, expensive but ill-considered tools to solve communications problems. These problems don't always warrant such a costly, high-fidelity solution. But even when they do merit that kind of solution, insufficient intention and energy go into creating the meeting experience itself.

> *If you are feeling like there's no agenda and not sure why everyone is there, you're likely not the only one.*
>
> **—CARRIE HANE**
> **DIGITAL COMMUNICATIONS STRATEGY COACH, TANZEN**

A lack of a clearly defined agenda is a symptom of the problem, but designing a meeting means more than just having an agenda. The problem is that meetings aren't considered in the same way that designers consider problems they are trying to solve. That's what "designing a meeting" is all about: thinking about your meetings as though you were a designer.

Thinking like a designer means taking an iterative, cyclical approach—an approach that mixes in research and testing of concepts. Using a basic design process as a checklist for planning and evaluating meetings is how this is done. This design process approach, credited to Tim Brown,[1] describes four discrete steps that turn an ordinary process for making something into one that leads to a more positive outcome.

1. Clearly define the problem that a design should solve through observation and good old-fashioned research.

2. Create and consider multiple options, as opposed to sticking to a single solution.

3. Select the option assumed to be the best and begin an iterative effort to refine it from a minimum viable concept. This contrasts with spending excessive time visualizing the finished product in every gory detail.

4. Execute or "ship" at an agreed-upon level of fidelity so that you have an opportunity to see how the design fares in the real world with real people. After that, jump back to step one as needed.

This design process has led to countless innovations in all aspects of our lives. It is often credited as the process that allowed disruptive *and* successful ideas to emerge in the market. But imagine your workplace culture—perhaps you work for a large corporation with hundreds (or hundreds of thousands) of employees that engage in many ceremonial meetings, based upon hierarchy, tradition, and previous but unsustainable successes. Or you might work for a small, nimble, start-up business of just a few smart people, who only assemble when there is a shared sense of necessity.

On either side of that spectrum, it is likely that the organization isn't thinking about the specific jobs that each meeting should perform. Applying those four steps of the design process to meetings themselves

1. Tim Brown, *Change by Design* (New York: HarperCollins, 2009).

provides a framework for evaluating if an existing meeting is perform-
. ing adequately. You can apply them to a single, important meeting in
order to design it better, or use the steps to evaluate, improve, or even
eliminate recurring meetings, such as a standing check-in for a project
team, like the one Jim had with the vice presidents from the beginning
of the chapter.

Apply Design Thinking to Existing Meetings

We'll call Jim's cross-disciplinary team on Rocket Design's big project
"Team Rocket." Team Rocket just made it through a difficult design
effort and presented their final efforts in the form of a series of screens.
The team includes product managers, user interface designers, front-
end and back-end developers, some marketing or social media folks,
and a part-time business analyst. They may or may not work in a formal
agile style—it doesn't really matter.

The team is in bad shape after that meeting, from lots of disagreements
over the final product, long hours, and disappointed stakeholders. The
designs are perceived as being behind the curve compared to their
competitors' efforts, despite Team Rocket having strong feelings to the
contrary. They decide to institute a new recurring meeting to "prevent
things from getting out of hand in the future."

> *Recognize where your meeting habits come from, and if they
> are truly still working.*
>
> **—DAVID SLEIGHT**
> **DESIGN DIRECTOR, PROPUBLICA**

When you get busy, your calendar is littered with recurring team
meetings, also known as *standing meetings* or *check-ins*. They are the
mosquitoes of meetings. They seem to be myriad, and each one takes a
little bit of your life away, but not enough to kill you; just enough to be

a nuisance. For each one of these meetings, you should always have two questions in the back of your mind:

- Why did you establish this meeting?
- Has that job been done?

If you can't answer the first, or the second answer is "yes," the meeting should be deleted or declined. It's that simple. Part of knowing when a standing meeting like Team Rocket's course correction meeting is working is recognizing when it's time to stop having it. Continuing to expect a productive outcome out of the same get-together when the goals have already been achieved (or new goals haven't been clearly articulated) is a special kind of insanity that only exists in meetings. To combat that insanity, apply the design-thinking checklist.

1. Identify the problem the meeting is intended to solve. Understand that problem sufficiently with research or a clear understanding of constraints.

2. Revisit and experiment with format, including length of time and method of facilitation. Consider skipping a few meetings, just to see what happens.

3. Make changes to the meeting semi-permanent after observing successes. Eliminate changes that don't produce successes.

4. Walk away from meetings that no longer do the job intended.

Identify the Problem

Team Rocket's identification of the problem is painfully vague. Preventing "things" from getting "out of hand" is going to mean different things to different team members. Which things? What is the threshold for "out of hand?"

In the hope of making a group of people more collaborative, people throw meetings at problems without sufficiently examining the problem itself. A regular meeting is an expensive way to solve a vague problem (see Figure 1.1), because meetings cost as much as everyone's combined paycheck for the allotted time. If the goal is to get people talking, there are much cheaper tools than meetings. Instant messaging tools such as Slack,[2] Hipchat,[3] and even good old-fashioned email allow groups of people to communicate a tremendous amount of information asynchronously, making it "knowledge on demand." Tools like these can reduce unnecessary face time used for communication *if* they are applied with a clear purpose. Here's an example of what I mean by "clear purpose":

"We use (chat platform/channel) to discuss daily tasks and request assistance. Post your awesome cat pictures or recipes somewhere else."

FIGURE 1.1 Meetings can be pretty costly when we are unprepared, because it's everyone's paycheck.

2. Slack, https://slack.com/
3. Hipchat, http://hipchat.com/

If you still need a meeting, the problem needs to be defined. When the problem feels under (or even un-) defined, identify and agree on the problem the meeting is intended to solve. Then diagnose the problem. Can anyone in your group be specific about what a check-in meeting is intended to accomplish? If they can, that's a good start.

Job performance indicators for Team Rocket's standing meeting could include an increase in efficiency by reducing the number of steps in a process, a list of ways in which the designs can be "ahead of the curve," or the amount of new ideas produced around current problems reported by people receiving food delivery. Each of these goals is measurable, establishing a baseline against which the meeting can be examined.

Working from a primary problem, you can identify secondary problems, such as identifying and routinizing successful processes, or confronting individual fears about what could go wrong if Team Rocket weren't doing its job well. Focusing on what could go wrong also has the potential to repair a negative project culture by providing a transparent forum for building camaraderie and trust.

A meeting is a synchronous approach to communication. It takes full advantage of the ways in which human beings communicate via speech, intentional and unintentional body language, and manipulation of physical space, such as creating a diagram together. A meeting affords tremendous capabilities for communication, but not all problems require this much communication to address. Once you have an agreement about the intended outcome, you've take the first step toward designing better meetings. The next step is running some experiments.

Consider Multiple Formats

Team Rocket is trying to position their design work and their client as groundbreaking in the competitive market of online meal delivery. A positive outcome of the ongoing meeting could be measured by the amount of agency (or client) blog posts around unique functionality, as it's being developed. They are currently producing up to two blog posts per week, but that output isn't fast enough to keep up with the conversation. Each time they meet, they talk at length about this problem, and then they talk some more.

A conversation is only one of several ways to structure this team's time. Sadly, most meetings lean heavily on talking and only talking. Instead of talking, they could try collaboratively visualizing the process of getting a blog post published in a flow chart on the wall. A wall diagram, as seen in Figure 1.2, shows how visualizing a process in sequence can reveal efficiency gains by examining and questioning individual steps to publication. Physical objects that can be manipulated, such as sticky notes, can catalog options—pros and cons. What about even spending some time without speaking, where ideas are written and shared *before* being discussed?

FIGURE 1.2 Sticky notes create models to visualize discussion.

Productive meetings increase clarity about a problem, identify tactics to solve a problem, and evaluate the relative merit of those tactics. Sometimes conversation can get the job done, but constraints presented by the human brain are often inaccurate and too subjective.

See Chapter 2, "The Design Constraint of All Meetings," for an overview of these problems.

Exclusively relying on conversation and human memory is a single pattern for executing a meeting, and often a faulty pattern that creates disagreement where none may exist. There are other patterns for facilitation and capture. You'll find them throughout the book, with most residing in Chapters 3, 4, and 5: "Build Agendas Out of Ideas, People, and Time," "Manage Conflict with Facilitation," and "Facilitation Strategy and Style."

If you've started exploring other options, the next step is to pick the options that sound promising and start making some changes.

Make Small Changes and Assess Improvements

What if Team Rocket never changed their meeting format? Sticking to a meeting format without further experimentation is like flying on auto-pilot: it only works for a limited amount of time. Symptoms of autopilot meetings include the same, strong personalities repeatedly driving the agenda and people tuning out, agreeing to whatever runs out the clock. Worst of all, the autopilot meeting loses sight of its original intention. With iterative changes over time, a regularly scheduled standing meeting can be tweaked to balance contributions and use structured collaboration to reclaim precious work time.

Team Rocket might experiment by introducing time limits for individual speakers. In certain corners of Google, time limits have proven to be one of the single most effective methods of keeping meetings aligned to decision-making.[4] The ruthlessness of a simple countdown clock keeps

4. Jillian D'Onfro, "Google Ventures Found the Secret to Productive Meetings in a First Grade Classroom," *Business Insider,* June 30, 2014, http://www.businessinsider.com/google-ventures-time-management-trick-2014-6

comments on task (see Figure 1.3), warning the group when someone is running out of time to speak. Meetings with this tool start closer to the scheduled time and finish ahead of time. As suggested previously, writing before speaking within a target length, such as a single sentence, also encourages people to consider what they say before they say it.

FIGURE 1.3 Some departments at Google use a simple timer, called the *time timer*, to keep meetings on track.

Without questioning (and measuring) performance, standing meetings fall into autopilot, or worse, disrepair. Staying open to refinements of what is already taking place within an ongoing status meeting avoids these problems. But eventually, all recurring meetings must end, which is the last step in the process of designing a meeting.

Know When the Job Is Done

After adding a countdown clock and using sticky notes to visualize their process, Team Rocket has been able to increase the number of cutting-edge feature announcements they make about their work. They decide to discontinue the meeting, and feel damn good about that decision.

Walking away from something that has done its job feels great. Agreement about how long a standing meeting is going to be in place can be reached by following that design thinking process through to its natural conclusion: research and understand the problem, try multiple agenda protocols, and iterate or tweak the format until the job is done.

A Better Definition of "Meeting"

Habits are the result of behaviors becoming separated from an awareness of the intentions behind those behaviors. When habits form as parts of the process of working together, such as standing meetings, those meetings start to be labeled with descriptions, rather than ascribed with purpose. They are "where the team gathers," or "when we talk about the project," or simply "that thing we do on Tuesday." When you apply a design process to meetings, you reconnect getting together with having a reason to do it.

Consider the very next meeting that you're about to have. Do you have doubts about its value? Ask yourself, or your team, two simple questions about that meeting. These questions will help you define its job in a way that reconnects it to a larger purpose.

- What is the outcome this meeting will enable?
- How can you measure that outcome?

That's a simpler, better definition for a meeting. A meeting is something that enables us to achieve an outcome that we can't otherwise achieve without it, measured in an agreed-upon fashion. We don't call a car "that thing with wheels and seats," even though it's as accurate of a definition as "that thing we do on Tuesday." If you've got the money for gas and maintenance, a car is the freedom to relocate yourself. A meeting is a mechanism for creating meaningful change in your work.

WHAT YOU NEED TO KNOW

People will call new meetings or continue to have existing ones because they're upset about a previous failure, or they fear a future one. As a result, meeting agendas get stuck in a very small part of the design process loop: considering and applying a single approach. That stagnation crowds calendars with standing meetings and leads them into standing boredom and standing confusion. To alleviate that stagnation, apply a design process to meetings with the following four steps.

1. Identify the problem that the meeting is intended to solve and research the problem before committing to a meeting.

2. Consider more than one approach to a meeting.

3. Make small changes to a meeting based on observed improvements or failures.

4. Know when the meeting has done its job and then walk away from it.

By asking these questions, you should be able to figure out when a standing meeting is a good idea and when it isn't. Once you're sure a meeting is going to do the trick, the next step is to take a hard look at what a meeting is composed of and start iterating and making those small changes.

> *We don't reflect on our collaboration nearly enough. How could we have worked together better? How could we have gotten to this outcome sooner? What was a good use of our time? Where did it sort of drag on? We need to actually sit down and take it apart.*
>
> **—JARED SPOOL**
> **MAKER OF AWESOMENESS, CENTER CENTRE AND UIE**

CONTINUES ➤

CONTINUED ➤

In case it wasn't obvious, this approach applies to any kind of meeting. It illustrates the differences between the problems a single meeting (or series of meetings) is intended to solve and the larger intentions of a project, or even an organization. It goes without saying that those intentions vary greatly based on the kind of work, the position within the organizational hierarchy, and the organizational culture. These are the constraints placed upon meetings, which are explored more extensively in the following chapters. However, before considering multiple approaches, you need to do step one, which is to understand the problem as bounded by its constraints. And there's one constraint that all meetings share, which you'll learn about in the next chapter.

2

The Design Constraint of All Meetings

J ane is a "do it right, or I'll do it myself" kind of person. She leads marketing, customer service, and information technology teams for a small airline that operates between islands of the Caribbean. Her work relies heavily on "reservation management system" (RMS) software, which is due for an upgrade. She convenes a Monday morning meeting to discuss an upgrade with the leadership from each of her three teams. The goal of this meeting is to identify key points for a proposal to upgrade the outdated software.

Jane begins by reviewing the new software's advantages. She then goes around the room, engaging each team's representatives in an open discussion. They capture how this software should alleviate current pain points; someone from marketing takes notes on a laptop, as is their tradition. The meeting lasts nearly three hours, which is a lot longer than expected, because they frequently loop back to earlier topics as people forget what was said. It concludes with a single follow-up action item: the director of each department will provide her with two lists for the upgrade proposal. First, a list of cost savings, and second, a list of timesaving outcomes. Each list is due back to Jane by the end of the week.

The first team's list is done early but not organized clearly. The second list provides far too much detail to absorb quickly, so Jane puts their work aside to summarize later. By the end of the following Monday, there's no list from the third team—it turns out they thought she meant the *following* Friday. Out of frustration, Jane calls another meeting to address the problems with the work she received, which range from "not quite right" to "not done at all." Based on this pace, her upgrade proposal is going to be finished two weeks later than planned.

What went wrong? The plan seemed perfectly clear to Jane, but each team remembered their marching orders differently, if they remembered them at all. Jane *could* have a meeting experience that helps her team form more accurate memories. But for that meeting to happen, she needs to understand *where* those memories are formed in her team and *how* to form them more clearly.

Better Meetings Make Better Memories

If people are the one ingredient that all meetings have in common, there is one design constraint they all bring: their capacity to remember the discussion. That capacity lives in the human brain.

The brain shapes everything believed to be true about the world. On the one hand, it is a powerful computer that can be trained to memorize thousands of numbers in random sequences.[1] But brains are also easily deceived, swayed by illusions and pre-existing biases. Those things show up in meetings as your instincts. Instincts vary greatly based on differences in the amount and type of previous experience. The paradox of ability and deceive-ability creates a weird mix of unpredictable behavior in meetings. It's no wonder that they feel awkward.

What is known about how memory works in the brain is constantly evolving. To cover that in even a little detail is beyond the scope of this book, so this chapter is not meant to be an exhaustive look at human memory. However, there are a few interesting theories that will help you be more strategic about how you use meetings to support forming actionable memories.

Your Memory in Meetings

The brain's job in meetings is to accept inputs (things we see, hear, and touch) and store it as memory, and then to apply those absorbed ideas in discussion (things we say and make). See Figure 2.1.

FIGURE 2.1 The human brain has a diverse set of inputs that contribute to your memories.

1. Joshua Foer, *Moonwalking with Einstein* (New York: Penguin Books, 2011).

Neuroscience has identified four theoretical stages of memory, which include sensory, working, intermediate, and long-term. Understanding working memory and intermediate memory is relevant to meetings, because these stages represent the most potential to turn thought into action.

Working Memory

You may be familiar with the term *short-term memory*. Depending on the research you read, the term *working memory* has replaced *short-term memory* in the vocabulary of neuro- and cognitive science. I'll use the term *working memory* here. Designing meeting experiences to support the working memory of attendees will improve meetings.

Working memory collects around 30 seconds of the things you've recently heard and seen. Its storage capacity is limited, and that capacity varies among individuals. This means that not everyone in a meeting has the same capacity to store things in their working memory. You might assume that because *you* remember an idea mentioned within the last few minutes of a meeting, everyone else probably will as well. That is not necessarily the case.

You can accommodate variations in people's ability to use working memory by establishing a reasonable pace of information. The pace of information is directly connected to how well aligned attendees' working memories become. To make sure that everyone is on the same page, you should set a pace that is deliberate, consistent, and slower than your normal pace of thought.

Sometimes, concepts are presented more quickly than people can remember them, simply because the presenter is already familiar with the details. Breaking information into evenly sized, consumable chunks is what separates a great presenter from an average (or bad) one. In a meeting, slower, more broken-up pacing allows a group of people to engage in constructive and critical thinking more effectively. It gets the same ideas in everyone's head. (For a more detailed dive into the pace of content in meetings, see Chapter 3, "Build Agendas Out of Ideas, People, and Time.")

Theoretical models that explain working memory are complex, as seen in Figure 2.2.[2] This model presumes two distinct processes taking place in your brain to make meaning out of what you see, what you hear, and how much you can keep in your mind. Assuming that your brain creates working memories from what you see and what you hear in different ways, *combining* listening and seeing in meetings becomes more essential to getting value out of that time.

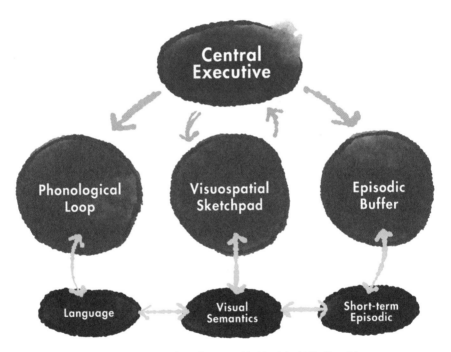

FIGURE 2.2 Alan Baddeley and Graham Hitch's Model of Working Memory provides context for the interplay between what we see and hear in meetings.

2. A. D. Baddeley and G. Hitch, "Working Memory," in *The Psychology of Learning and Motivation: Advances in Research and Theory*, ed. G. H. Bower (New York: Academic Press, 1974), 8:47–89.

In a meeting, absorbing something seen and absorbing something heard require different parts of the brain. Those two parts can work *together* to improve retention (the quantity and accuracy of information in our brain) or *compete* to reduce retention. Nowhere is this better illustrated than in the research of Richard E. Meyer, where he has found that "people learn better from words and pictures than from words alone, but not all graphics are created equal(ly)."[3] When what you hear and what you see compete, it creates cognitive dissonance. Listening to someone speaking while reading the same words on a screen actually decreases the ability to commit something to memory. People who are subjected to presentation slides filled with speaking points face this challenge. But listening to someone while looking at a *complementary* photograph or drawing increases the likelihood of committing something to working memory.

Intermediate-Term Memory

Your memory should transform ideas absorbed in meetings into taking an action of some kind afterward. Triggering intermediate-term memories is the secret to making that happen. Intermediate-term memories last between two and three hours, and are characterized by processes taking place in the brain called *biochemical translation and transcription.* Translation can be considered as a process by which the brain makes new meaning. Transcription is where that meaning is replicated (see Figures 2.3a and 2.3b). In both processes, the cells in your brain are creating new proteins using existing ones: making some "new stuff" from "existing stuff."[4]

3. Richard E. Meyer, "Principles for Multimedia Learning with Richard E. Mayer," Harvard Initiative for Learning & Teaching (blog), July 8, 2014, http://hilt.harvard.edu/blog/principles-multimedia-learning-richard-e-mayer
4. M. A. Sutton and T. J. Carew, "Behavioral, Cellular, and Molecular Analysis of Memory in Aplysia I: Intermediate-Term Memory," *Integrative and Comparative Biology* 42, no. 4 (2002): 725–735.

Fig a.

Fig b.

FIGURE 2.3 Biochemical translation (a) and transcription (b), loosely in the form of understanding a hat.

Here's an example: instead of having someone take notes on a laptop, imagine if Jane sketched a diagram that helped her make sense out of the discussion, using what was stored in her working memory. The creation of that diagram is an act of translation, and theoretically Jane should be able to recall the primary details of that diagram easily for two to three hours, because it's moving into her intermediate memory.

If Jane made copies of that diagram, and the diagram was so compelling that those copies ended up on everyone's wall around the office that would be transcription. Transcription is the (theoretical) process that leads us into longer-term stages of memory. Transcription connects understanding something within a meeting to acting on it later, well after the meeting has ended.

Most of the time simple meetings last from 10 minutes to an hour, while workshops and working sessions can last anywhere from 90 minutes to a few days. Consider the duration of various stages of memory against different meeting lengths (see Figure 2.4). A well-designed meeting experience moves the right information from working to intermediate memory. Ideas generated and decisions made should materialize into actions that take place outside the meeting. Any session without breaks that lasts longer than 90 minutes makes the job of your memories moving thought into action fuzzier, and therefore more difficult.

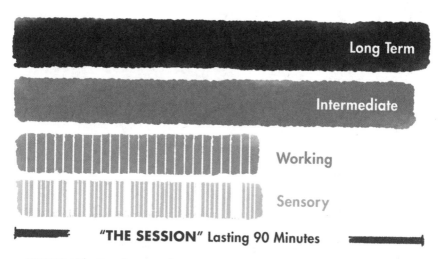

FIGURE 2.4 The time duration of common meetings against the varying durations for different stages of memory. Sessions longer than 90 minutes can impede memories from doing their job.

Jane's meeting with her three teams lasted nearly three hours. That length of time spent on a single task or topic taxes people's ability to form intermediate (actionable) memories. Action items become muddled, which leads to liberal interpretations of what each team is supposed to accomplish.

But just getting agreement about a shared task in the first place is a difficult design challenge. All stages of memory are happening simultaneously, with multiple translation and transcription processes being applied to different sounds and sights. A fertile meeting environment that accommodates multiple modes of input allows memories to form amidst the cognitive chaos.

Brain Input Modes

During a meeting, each attendee's brain in a meeting is either in a state of input or output. By choosing to assemble in a group, the assumption is implicit that information needs to be moved out of one place, or one brain, into another (or several others).

Some meetings, like presentations, move information in one direction. The goal is for a presenting party to move information from their brain to the brains in the audience. When you are presenting an idea, your brain is in output mode. You use words and visuals to give form to ideas in the hopes that they will become memories in your audience. Your audience's brains are receiving information; if the presentation is well designed and well executed, their ears and their eyes will do a decent job of absorbing that information accurately.

In a live presentation, the output/input processes are happening synchronously. This is not like reading a written report or an email message, where the author (presenting party) has output information in absence of an audience, and the audience is absorbing information in absence of the author's presence; that is moving information asynchronously.

An energetic, collaborative meeting has the same input/output dynamic as a presentation, but there are two important distinctions. First, information is moving in two directions, not just one. Second, the movement between input and output states happens more frequently in smaller, faster bursts. Each brain in a fast-paced meeting is working to absorb the information from surrounding brains while also outputting information for the cumulative benefit of the group. In the best of circumstances, that should increase clarity about a problem or solution and culminate in a shared understanding that wouldn't exist without everyone.

A meeting is a system that facilitates knowledge input and output while having the potential to create new perspectives at the same time. Poor meetings don't move ideas from one brain to another effectively, and therefore do a worse job at developing interesting or useful new ideas. Good ones move information more quickly and provide space for unexpected new ideas. Good meetings happen more often when you accommodate attendees' varying abilities to listen, to learn, and to express ideas in a way that's "brain consumable." You can build on what you've learned about the way people remember things to design better avenues for input.

More Effective Listening

You spend most meetings, especially ones called in haste, using your ears as the primary mode of input for getting information (see Figure 2.5). Groups regularly fall back on conversation as the modus operandi. As a result, listening is the primary input mode for meetings.

Another place that you have done a lot of listening, hopefully, is in the classroom. Students spend anywhere from 12 to 20 years of their lives in a classroom, hearing daily or weekly lectures from a teacher or professor. Like meetings, lectures also rely on hearing as a primary mode of input for building memories. But the effectiveness of listening at creating good memories in lectures has been studied, and the results aren't pretty. In his book *What's the Use of Lectures*, Donald Bligh demonstrated that students in a lecture audience have a heart rate that is in constant decline, decreasing energy and focus.[5] After about 20 to 30 minutes, people begin to have difficulty absorbing information via listening. Being at rest, bodies have a hard time maintaining sufficient energy to learn.

FIGURE 2.5 Listening is the mechanism used most often for absorbing information in meetings.

Think about how the experience of a meeting accommodates that loss of energy over time. You probably use calendaring software to distribute invitations to meetings, manage group availability, and document meetings that have taken place. Despite accommodating custom lengths, calendaring software interfaces default to 30- and 60-minute blocks by design.

When there are more than 30 minutes of straight listening to do, but 30 minutes are all that a reasonable brain can handle, that's a problem. To account for this, try to break the meeting content into 20- to 30-minute durations. Within each 20- to 30-minute session, include time to reflect on what participants have heard. That reflection can take the form of conversation with the presenter, conversation with

5. Donald Bligh, *What's the Use of Lectures* (San Francisco: Jossey-Bass, 2000).

one another, or applying the knowledge in an exercise. Establishing a rhythm based on stages of memory improves listening as an input strategy for meetings.

Jane's proposal planning meeting could have been more effectively structured as a single 90-minute meeting with three 30-minute sections. Each 30-minute component could focus on a single department's lists, with the first 10 minutes on list one (dollar savings), the next 10 minutes on list two (time savings), and the last 10 minutes on reflection of those lists. Having all departments present for each other's discussions would add value by eliminating redundant list items in real time.

> *Time constraints on workshop activities help people ignore their inner critic.*
>
> **—ELLEN DE VRIES**
> **CONTENT STRATEGIST, CLEARLEFT LTD**

The inner critic to which Ellen de Vries refers can rear its head as "imposter syndrome." With too much time to focus on a single issue in a discussion, you might start to believe that you have nothing to say because you aren't qualified to contribute, despite evidence to the contrary. This behavior is documented in psychological studies,[6] and can be discouraged in discussions by simply preventing people from having too much time to spend in a single thought space. Aggressive time constraints encourage people to act more quickly and use the limited brain energy they have in powerful bursts.

Those bursts need to be refueled. You can create energy in longer meetings and workshops by feeding the brain with food. With extensive workshop facilitation experience and the help of conversations with a few nutritionists, Margot Bloomstein has some thoughts on how to keep workshops intellectually productive for extended periods of time.

6. P. R. Clance and S. A. Imes, "The Imposter Phenomenon in High Achieving Women: Dynamics and Therapeutic Intervention," *Psychotherapy: Theory, Research and Practice* 15, no. 3 (1978): 241–247.

WHAT SHOULD PEOPLE EAT DURING A MEETING?

Margot Bloomstein
Principal, Appropriate, Inc.

Margot is the author of Content Strategy at Work *and a principal of Appropriate, Inc., a brand and content strategy consultancy. For more than 15 years, she has shaped communication for brands like Fidelity, Harvard, Lindt & Sprüngli, and Lovehoney. She keynotes conferences and leads workshops worldwide.*

Twice a week, every week, during my first semester of college, I would wake up in a history lecture. I'd jerk awake to the squeak of chalk or a crescendo in the professor's delivery and then scramble to understand what was going on. This isn't a story of amnesia or abduction—I meant to be in that lecture, and I wanted to pay close attention. I knew where I was. But I didn't fully understand how I got to that point: I didn't grasp why I invariably always fell asleep 15 minutes into that class.

Eating and Listening

Step away from the packed, toasty lecture hall, and it's easy to see why I had such a tough time staying awake and giving the class the attention and rigor it deserved. I was a dutiful, attentive student—when my eyes were open. After my morning studio classes ended, I would meet friends in the cafeteria. Living on my own for the first time and still enjoying a revved-up teenage metabolism, I would often down a couple of grilled cheese sandwiches or that day's pasta entrée, and maybe finish off the meal with an ice cream cone. Occasionally, I'd grab an apple or soda on my way out, then stroll across campus to my history class, which met at 1:30.

I walked into that class with big plans to learn and engage, but in reality I brought much more: specifically, 90 plus grams of fast-acting carbohydrates, and that's not even counting the soda that came in with me.

CONTINUES ➤

CONTINUED ➤

Other than the two slices of American cheese between highly refined white bread, there wasn't much protein or fat in my body to slow down the absorption of those carbohydrates. My brain was getting bathed in sweet, sweet glucose and was promptly lulled to sleep.

Some tough love in nutrition and its effect on my GPA helped me reevaluate what I was eating and how it affected my capability to learn. I don't remember much from that history class, but I took away some important lessons that affect how I teach, facilitate, and organize workshops today.

Food That Does a Meeting Good

In addition to structuring what participants will do and learn, I pay close attention to what they'll eat and when they eat it. In morning meetings, I want people to arrive ready to focus—and not just on their own grumbling stomachs or anxiety about the nearest coffee shop. Also, I want *everyone* to be able to fully engage. No workshop or meeting should include people not vital to its outcome. So if all participants are important, that means vegetarian participants, participants on calorie- or carbohydrate-restricted diets, and people with gluten or other allergies are all important and deserve good food that meets their needs.

Good food isn't just *any* food. Heed my plight with the grilled cheese sandwiches! If you want people to bring their best energy and maintain engagement following a meal, plan to give them the right nutrients to sustain that energy level. That's not just coffee washed down with more coffee. In consulting with nutritionists, I've learned that we rely on simple carbohydrates for a *quick* source of energy. If you've ever downed a candy bar or a can of soda, you've felt the sugar rush. But when you didn't chase it with something more substantial, you probably felt an energy crash soon after. Simple carbohydrates, like juice, soda, and refined sugars in white bread and pastries, will do that to you.

If you want food that creates and maintains energy, take advantage of how the stomach "layers" nutrients for absorption. We metabolize food components at different rates, but by mixing them, we slow the absorption and minimize spikes in blood sugar. Fat and protein slow the absorption of carbohydrates so that your body can draw on that glucose over several hours, rather than burn through it in mere minutes. What food should you offer workshop participants?

Morning Meetings

At breakfast meetings, skip the pastries in favor of prepared scrambled eggs. Offer bagels with peanut butter: carbohydrates slowed by a source of fat and protein! Premade breakfast burritos that incorporate avocado and black beans are another tasty source of healthy fat and protein. Yogurt with no added sugar meets many dietary needs, too, combining carbohydrates, protein, and minimal fat in one convenient, single-serving container.

Mid-day Meetings

To head off a post-lunch slump, again, put biology to work on your behalf. Put together a menu with more complex carbohydrates by trading white bread for whole wheat on the sandwiches—the longer those carbohydrate chains are, the more time they take to break down. Ensure that everyone, regardless of their dietary restrictions, can find sources of protein.

Afternoon Meetings

Later in the afternoon consider more nutrient-rich snacks than the ubiquitous cookie plate. Trail mix with dried fruit and nuts, yogurt cups, a communal cheese plate, or a raw vegetable platter can help everyone focus and engage with the content.

If you want your audience there, remember, you want them present—and that means you want their energy and attention throughout your time together.

Providing reasonably paced content and refueling with appropriate food will improve listening in meetings. But better listening alone is not enough. Studies of teaching strategies have proven that people learn across multiple mediums. The concept of multimedia learning is based on the cognitive theory of multi-modal perception, which covers how you make sense of the world around you using all available senses.[7] Your brain finds more meaning by combining listening with seeing or with touch. The degree to which that meaning is accurate can be increased (or decreased) by the interactions that take place between different "modes" of information consumption.

There are lots of ways that the interplay of learning modes can trick you. Ventriloquists use visual perception to change auditory perception by creating the illusion that a human voice is coming from a wooden puppet. Human brains are *predisposed* to visual input being perceived as dominant; if what you see contradicts what you hear, you are more likely to believe what you see. So how does the brain "see" information in meetings, and how can you use sight to build better memories?

Visual Listening

Visualization is a surprisingly effective method of getting memories into your brain (see Figure 2.6). In his book *Moonwalking with Einstein*, Joshua Foer summarizes studies that demonstrate when shown an image, your brain has a nearly infallible ability to know whether or not it's been seen previously.[8] This fact applies to a small set of images or thousands of images, and it works over extended periods of time. But keep in mind (pun intended) that memory is still unreliable and can be exhausted— this is the design constraint all meetings face. Creating and reinforcing memories with visuals can manage and even reduce this constraint.

7. Richard E. Meyer, "Principles for Multimedia Learning with Richard E. Mayer," Harvard Initiative for Learning & Teaching (blog), July 8, 2014, http://hilt.harvard.edu/blog/principles-multimedia-learning-richard-e-mayer

8. Joshua Foer, *Moonwalking with Einstein* (New York: Penguin Books, 2011).

FIGURE 2.6 Visualization as an input mechanism can be used far more effectively in most meetings.

Whiteboarding an idea (visualizing it publicly) allows a group to point at the same thing and say "yes," or "no."

—DANA CHISNELL
CODIRECTOR, CENTER FOR CIVIC DESIGN

Someone who takes notes in meetings can be called a *scribe* or a *meeting secretary*. They transcribe the discussion at a nearly impossible level of detail, and if you're lucky they make those notes available to attendees. In most organizations, the notes are rarely revisited. You leave a meeting focused on the tasks that apply exclusively to you. Once you feel like you've got those tasks down, you aren't likely to reread meeting notes. Those notes disappear in the piles of email messages that are there to make you feel better, but don't really add to the quality of our work.

Stop taking notes in meetings this way, now and forever.

Give the scribe a different job: get those notes in front of everyone's eyes at the same time, in real time while the discussion is happening. While people are engaged in talking (or for our purposes, "auditory input and output"), the scribe creates a visual record of only the main ideas, the conflicts, and the decisions on the wall. It needs to be large enough so that anyone in the room can read it from wherever they are sitting. That way, when the scribe captures something incorrectly, someone in the meeting can speak up and provide a correction.

Attendees in this scenario see the conversation unfold visually before them. It creates a feedback loop verifying accuracy between what people hear and see. They don't have to engage in both all the time, but switching between listening and looking modes becomes possible when it suits the individual. Miss something? Look at the wall, or the screen if you are meeting with a distributed group. Suddenly, meeting notes accommodate multiple input modes, as well as create a central point of focus.

For example, Jane's meeting was missing visualized discussion. She relied exclusively on listening to get the same action item into everyone's mind. A public note taker could have visualized those lists in real time by pulling the parts of the conversation out that fit into each list. Leaving the meeting with that visual would have clearly aligned all three teams on what each list was for, and where different savings they anticipated should go. Jane's teams would have provided documentation that reduced Jane's extra effort, as opposed to increasing it, because the structure of the list would have been more clearly defined in their memories.

The practice of visual facilitation is a little beyond just note taking. It involves using simple visuals and sketches to represent ideas. It's practiced by accomplished facilitators worldwide, and there are regular conferences dedicated to its practice. Compared to words, a diagram or sketch conveys more information without much additional effort. Concepts of time, connection, disconnection, emotion, and more can be represented more quickly with lines, boxes, arrows, and simple facial drawings. For more on visual approaches facilitation, make sure that you read Chapter 5, "Facilitation Strategy and Style."

Getting in Touch with Your Ideas

Touching other people during a meeting? Probably not a good idea. But physically manipulating objects during a discussion is a *great* idea. Moving yourself and moving tools that you can hold in your hands provides a platform for interactions between people and ideas (see Figure 2.7). It's another great input mode for creating understanding between people on complex ideas in less time.

FIGURE 2.7 Using manipulated objects, or manipulatives, is another effective input method.

The meeting tactics that (are) the most reusable are easy to follow and tactile, requiring manipulation of things in physical (or virtual) spaces.

—JAMES BOX AND ELLEN DE VRIES
DIRECTOR OF USER EXPERIENCE, CLEARLEFT LTD (BOX) &
CONTENT STRATEGIST, CLEARLEFT LTD (DE VRIES)

The most common example of an easily manipulated object, or a "manipulative," is the sticky note. These notes provide the ability to create and absorb information structures more easily by arranging ideas in physical space. Sticky notes work well in meetings because they engage the part of your brain that interprets meaning from spatial relationships. So...move things around in your meetings! The act of getting moving applies Baddeley's working memory model into the conference room. When you arrange sticky notes on a wall or modify a physical, cardboard prototype with scissors and glue, you are building the "visuospatial sketchpad" in the real world (see Figure 2.8).

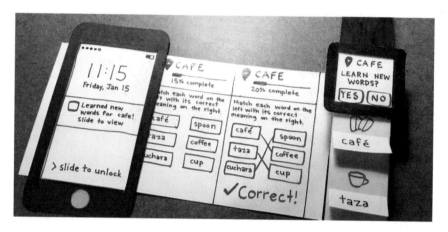

FIGURE 2.8 A simple, made-with-scissors-marker-and-paper kindergarten-style prototype from Amy Mae Roberts, Product Designer, Microsoft.

Visualizations in meetings are living records. Continued interaction with those records will create better memories. While extending Baddeley's research, Logie posited that the visuospatial sketchpad is broken into two different parts.[9] A "visual cache" stores information about form and color, while the "inner scribe" deals with movement and position in space. Different parts of the brain are working together to do a better job of committing things to your memory, using a visual metaphor.

9. R. H. Logie, *Visuo-Spatial Working Memory* (Hove, UK: Psychology Press, 1995).

Getting ideas into your brain effectively therefore also means moving them *out* of the meeting, as a shared public record, so that you can continue to act upon those ideas. Unlike meeting notes you take on a laptop, visualized records of a conversation can be revisited and iterated upon after the meeting is over. That continued engagement with a visual record will pull more of the brain into the work. The more engaged each of these parts of the brain become, the more likely that successful memory creation, synthesis, and application will happen. The stuff discussed in a meeting gets done, and it gets done correctly.

Putting the Brain to Work for Jane's Meeting

Everything you perceive to be real in the world happens as input into your brain. By considering the brain as the primary design constraint for a meeting, you engineer powerful learning experiences, focus teams on the right aspects of projects, and accommodate different modes of input within a meeting.

Remember Jane and her three teams at the Caribbean airline? By taking advantage of visual capture via Post-it Notes, she could break the ideas for each of the two lists (time savings and cost savings) into a wall-sized representation of the lists themselves. These lists could be created, at least in part, during the meeting. Distributing a photo of the results of the meeting wall immediately afterward would provide enough context for any additional work to be at the appropriate level of detail. Additional meetings could be eliminated, and Jane's team would have more clarity, because their memories would be more accurate.

WHAT YOU NEED TO KNOW

People, and specifically their brains, are a universal design constraint for meetings. The best way to design for this constraint is by creating ways to support more effective creation of memories. Here are several ways to make that happen:

- Working memory is the most active stage of memory in a meeting. It lasts on average 30 seconds, but it varies between individuals. You should cover information at a pace that is slower than you would normally use in a one-on-one conversation and break it into even chunks.

- Working memory has distinct ways in which it handles sights and sounds. Engage both by combining visuals with discussions in a complementary, not competing, style.

- The stage of memory that has the most capacity to create work after the meeting is intermediate memory. A meeting's length can interfere with keeping good intermediate memories if it is too long.

- The brain receives information in meetings via sound, sight, and touch inputs.

- People will listen better (and form stronger memories) by breaking content into 20- to 30-minute presentations, activities, or interactions. Each interaction should also include time for discussion of what was learned. This helps move working memories into intermediate ones.

- Eating healthy fats and proteins will do a better job of sustaining people's attention in longer meetings than donuts and cookies.

- Creating and reinforcing memories with visuals are great ways to activate part of the brain that isn't otherwise possible. Visual facilitation is the practice of exclusively using sketching to facilitate discussions, and it is an example of why simple visuals are uniquely effective.

- Objects you can physically manipulate, such as sticky notes and small physical prototypes, further empower the relationship between visualization and listening in the brain. These are called *manipulatives*.

3

Build Agendas
Out of Ideas,
People, and Time

D ave is an independent consultant who helps organizations figure out the relationship between how they organize information in digital products (websites, apps) and the job those products are intended to do. As an independent contractor, he adapts to the working culture of each client. Dave's latest client is a multinational insurance firm with inefficient design processes and an overworked in-house design team.

Dave scheduled a meeting to present six design principles he had developed to simplify the ongoing production work of the design team. The intention of the meeting was to build a shared understanding of these principles among the five members of the design team and the two senior stakeholders; he was not soliciting feedback for revisions. Dave restricted the agenda to around 10 minutes per principle. During each 10-minute session, he covered one or two examples of how each principle was applied. A brief period of time was reserved at the end of each 10-minute block for discussion. Here's what Dave's agenda looked like:

DAVE'S DESIGN PRINCIPLE AGENDA
- Review a principle (8 minutes)
- Discuss a principle (2 minutes)
- (Repeat six times, once for each principle)

It was a lot to cover. He expected to orient the team just enough to begin applying the principles in their work. Once they began to do so, Dave was on-hand to answer more questions via email.

Dave felt confident as the meeting was started. However, two minutes into the meeting, the CEO of the company, James, interrupted Dave with a question that belied a fundamental misunderstanding of the meeting's intent.

"On page 36 of the document, there's a blue button in the example diagram. Can that button be green?"

Jan, the Chief Design Officer, intervened, trying to help Dave.

"I think we're jumping ahead here, let's try to stay on topic. My team needs to be able to start applying these principles this week."

James replied:

"Well, I'm not sure I agree with the agenda of this meeting. I thought we were going to get a detailed review of the design of all of our different applications."

Jan disagreed:

"James, that would be a waste of time. We can read these documents on our own time. Let's use this time to explore how we could apply these principles on our own."

During the next 30 minutes, Dave was only able to get through a single design principle, due to continued interruptions from the two senior stakeholders. The remaining time was steamrolled by those stakeholders' continued debate regarding differing expectations of agendas. Sadly, Dave only went through two of the six principles he had planned to cover in the hour. He was unable to convey the intended ideas in the time allotted.

The Illusion of the Agenda

It sucks when you lose control of a meeting. In Dave's presentation, three different people had entered the meeting with three different agendas, and each agenda disrupted the other. Dave's agenda fell victim to a power struggle. Jan lost the benefits she had hoped to get for her design team. James' expectations were broken at the beginning, due to a lack of preparation on his part. Dave had distributed agendas in advance, and even personally emailed the "hippos" (**HI**ghest **P**aid **P**erson's **O**pinion) in the office to give them the opportunity to express additional expectations. But like a lot of busy people, James didn't have (or make) time to prepare. It's an excuse, but it's also a real design constraint that meetings face.

> *A well-designed agenda should work when it's "mostly broken."*
> *If unforeseen circumstances render an agenda impossible to*
> *execute, it was too brittle to begin with.*
>
> **—JAMES MACANUFO**
> **CREATIVE DIRECTOR, PIXEL PRESS AND COAUTHOR, GAMESTORMING**

Meeting derailments happen despite good intentions and solid preparation. It's frustrating when you put time and energy into preparing a plan that didn't work out. It feels disrespectful to you and the attendees who came prepared.

But all is not lost. The basic components that make up a meeting agenda are still present. The duration is not unlimited: there is a beginning, middle, and end. There are a quantifiable number of people present. Those people carry a limited set of expectations—ideas in their brains about why they showed up in the first place. Dave could have designed a better situation by not being tied to his agenda and instead prioritizing three things:

- What *ideas* did he intend to explore?
- How did the *people* in the room expect to receive those ideas (or were they expecting entirely different ideas)?
- How much *time* did he have to get through the material?

It's good to stay flexible about agendas, but important to be crystal clear about the three core elements of agenda building: ideas, people, and time. Sticking to these three elements, while being flexible about how you get there, keeps an agenda from being too brittle.

Count Your Ideas, Then Count Your People

The hour-long business meeting often ends up on your calendar because calendaring software (and the clock) defaults to that length of time. An hour is longer than necessary for a quick check-in, but depending on the group, it might not be long enough to fully explore many ideas or "just-complex-enough concepts." So, first, count how many of these you intend to address. That number gives you the ability to assess a meeting's scale.

How much information comprises a "just-complex-enough" concept? Here's an example—one of Dave's six design principles was "to keep the customer's eye on the ball." It's a common pitfall in software design to overwhelm users with too many options. To combat that tendency, Dave recommended that the most logical next step should be obvious on each screen. A single complex concept is simply a couple of sentences that describe a single piece of information—what you might fit on a sticky note (see Figure 3.1).

FIGURE 3.1 This much information is in a single, "just-complex-enough" concept.

It's not too difficult to keep in mind what Dave means when he says "keep the customer's eye on the ball." Now to put that idea into the context of a meeting, two people need to reach an agreement on that idea—to have the same meaning in their minds on which to base further conversation. Simple math dictates that there is a single point of agreement between two people. You might assume that for each additional person added to a group, you would add one more point of agreement. Unfortunately, it's not that simple.

For three people, those points of agreement jump to three; for five, they elevate to 10; and seven, they leap all the way up to 21. Crowded conversations of 12 people make getting everyone on the same page painfully difficult, as you can see by just counting the lines in Figure 3.2, illustrating a points-of-agreement model.

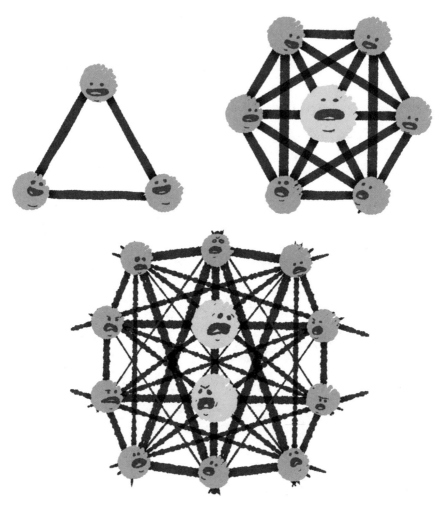

FIGURE 3.2 A points-of-agreement model, with three variations:
3 people: 3 points of agreement (Doable!)
7 people: 21 points of agreement (Overwhelming.)
12 people: 66 points of agreement (Nearly impossible!)

When you add one person to a meeting, you aren't just seeking that one person's new agreement. You are adding as many points of agreement as there are people who are already involved. Increasing the number of people in a meeting will scale up the complexity quickly. If you oversee a meeting's planning and can control who is being invited, start by capping it at six or seven people.

If more than seven people cannot be avoided or it's simply out of your hands, write down the reason that each person needs to be there in a simple statement. What is their anticipated goal? Make sure that each attendee knows your intention for inviting them. If you use calendaring software, include those intentions in the meeting invitation itself, or email each person what your take on their assumptions might be, just before the meeting, as a reminder. This will help them remember their role right before they join and get them in the correct frame of mind. You can revisit those expectations at the beginning of the conversation by writing them publicly before you get started.

The points-of-agreement model conveys the idea visually that adding more people makes the discussion more complex. This is one issue affecting Dave's unsuccessful presentation. Dave has eight people to deal with (including himself), and as you saw, some of those people have different expectations about the intentions of the meeting. Here's how Dave could have adjusted his agenda as soon as this became a problem: break into two smaller groups.

DAVE'S *ORIGINAL* DESIGN PRINCIPLE AGENDA

- Review a principle (8 minutes).
- Discuss a principle (2 minutes).
- (Repeat six times.)

DAVE'S *ADJUSTED* DESIGN PRINCIPLE AGENDA

- Identify two subgroups: a design group (design team) and a business outcomes group (leadership).
- Review a principle (8 minutes).
- Break into subgroups to discuss principle (2 minutes).
- (Repeat six times.)

By breaking into two groups, Dave isolates different expectations of the agenda (in this case, business outcomes versus design application efforts) to keep them from becoming distracting tangents at best and a derailing debate at worst.

Get to Know People

If there's a lot at stake for a meeting, different expectations can be explored with pre-meeting interviews. Dave had sent out agendas in advance, but he could also have spent time getting feedback on the agenda in one-on-one conversations. Conducting "meetings-before-the-meeting" is good for high-stakes meetings, especially when they are more complex workshops or intensive working sessions.

Advance interviews with attendees can make the difference between people getting the right story or the wrong one by previewing how much alignment exists among meeting participants. These interviews also provide content to build and supplement an agenda. You'll discover positive ways in which you can challenge your audience and where to push them out of their comfort zones. Use these basic guidelines when conducting pre-meeting interviews:

- Maintain an "off-the-record" and friendly tone.

- Find a personal connection to the interview subject early if possible. Look for shared background or interests, such as a city you've lived in or a sports team you like. If it's someone that you feel intimidated by, like a CEO, keep it light and general. Just don't force it or spend too much time on it; the goal is just to open a trusting connection.

- Gather specific expectations regarding the meeting's purpose and outcomes.

- Ask clear and direct questions, such as "What will this thing that we are building do? How does that help your business?"

Even with pre-interviews, you might find yourself in a group that is pursuing *too many* points of agreement, simply by covering too much information. Agendas can design against this tendency by adjusting the pace of information over time. How are complex concepts distributed over time to maximize absorption and meaningful discussion? There are ways to cover a lot of information in a shorter amount of time that work, and there are ways that will blow up in your face.

Scale Ideas to Time

I taught a college class for the first time in 2005. Having never taught before, I had to overcome my fear of getting in front of a group of people and learn how to talk productively for three hours each week. I had no idea how to structure what I knew into a learning experience that conveyed information efficiently and enjoyably.

I found a teaching expert with 30 years of experience teaching kids, adults, and even other teachers, both hands-on in the classroom and as an educational consultant. She even personally mentored the 2006 National Teacher of the Year award winner. If she hadn't also been my mother, I imagine she might have been too busy to speak with me. I asked her to teach me the basics of how to teach.

She shared two easy guidelines about how to scale ideas over time. Both are as applicable to boardrooms as they are to classrooms.

- People can only remember about seven or so complex concepts at a time, over a period of about 10 minutes. (It's a scientifically observed phenomenon, which George Miller called the "magical number seven plus or minus two."[1])

- Stop and review your previous seven (plus or minus two) concepts before moving to the next group every 10 minutes or so.

1. G. Miller, "The Magical Number Seven, Plus or Minus Two: Some Limits on Our Capacity for Processing Information," *Psychological Review* 63 (1956): 81–97.

Lectures and business meetings are mechanisms for conveying structured information. In both, not everyone is equally prepared (or inclined) to receive that information. People come into the room with a wide range of prior knowledge, and as we covered in Chapter 2, "The Design Constraint of All Meetings," a variable capacity for working memory.

You must structure content in the agenda to manage this challenge. Divide key concepts into groups of around seven items or fewer. I prefer five, because five is a number that has been more graspable in my experience. Five concepts at a time, with stopping points to review every 10 minutes or so, manages the cognitive load to accommodate variations in memory and expertise.

Apply "Groups of Five" in a Meeting

Beware of any argument when the speaker proclaims, "I will make my case with the following 15 points." That presentation isn't designed for you to find meaning and apply those ideas. Unless you're a tape recorder, it's difficult to remember that much at once; earlier points just trickle away. Just go to the grocery store without a long shopping list in hand and see how much you forget.

Slides with bulleted text are a common way to organize major points. You don't have to have slides with bullet points on them—you could just as easily put your points on a whiteboard or on a few notecards you have in your hand. But if you use slides, Miller's magic number is a good organizing principle for how much to put on a single slide at a time. Constrain yourself to around five, or ideally no more than seven items, on each slide (see Figure 3.3). After you go through each group of five concepts, lead the group in a review, discussion, or activity to apply what they have learned.

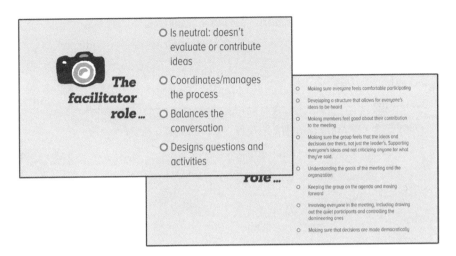

The facilitator role...

○ Is neutral: doesn't evaluate or contribute ideas

○ Coordinates/manages the process

○ Balances the conversation

○ Designs questions and activities

○ Making sure everyone feels comfortable participating

○ Developing a structure that allows for everyone's ideas to be heard

○ Making members feel good about their contribution to the meeting

○ Making sure the group feels that the ideas and decisions are theirs, not just the leader's. Supporting everyone's ideas and not criticizing anyone for what they've said.

○ Understanding the goals of the meeting and the organization

○ Keeping the group on the agenda and moving forward

○ Involving everyone in the meeting, including drawing out the quiet participants and controlling the domineering ones

○ Making sure that decisions are made democratically

FIGURE 3.3 Which of these slides can you process more easily?

There are many benefits to structuring content this way in a meeting. It reduces the opportunities for awkward moments, say when attendees interrupt for clarification or simply tune out. If you aren't in charge of a meeting but the pace of information is getting out of hand, you can still influence toward a more reasonable pace. Keep track of how many concepts have been covered and then *ask* to stop and review when you feel like you've hit the magic number. Those reviews reinforce ideas for the whole group. They also encourage the presenter to find stopping points and restructure things in a better way on the spot.

Dave's design principle agenda may have seemed well paced in this regard, but it wasn't. He had originally planned on reviewing a single complex concept every 10 minutes, but that didn't happen because there wasn't an agreed-upon scale of information as it pertained to each concept. What felt like a reasonable cognitive load for his attendees wasn't put into context relative to the full hour, from the beginning.

By changing his agenda to provide the principles in the beginning, Dave could assess a few things about his audience that would help him adjust the pace of the content as problems arose. Which principles have the most interest? Which are more difficult to convey? A simple review of the principles during the beginning of the meeting will reveal where the meeting is heading, driven by the assumptions and the intentions of its attendees.

DAVE'S *ORIGINAL* DESIGN PRINCIPLE AGENDA

- Review a principle (8 minutes).
- Discuss a principle (2 minutes).
- (Repeat six times.)

DAVE'S *ADJUSTED* DESIGN PRINCIPLE AGENDA

- Review all six principles (10 minutes).
- Review a single principle in more detail (6 to 7 minutes).
- Discuss a principle (2 minutes).
- (Repeat six times.)

When Groups of Five Aren't Enough

Hopefully, meetings will help you and your team to make important decisions. Sometimes those decisions are based on something that can't be boiled down to a group of five concepts. For example, Edward Tufte's critique of PowerPoint makes this clear by showing how oversimplification in presentations can weaken reasoning and lead to flawed decisions.[2] But that is no excuse to abandon good content structure in discussions.

Complicated information doesn't merit saying "We've got a lot to get through today, so let's dive right in." A machine-gun, rapid-fire format of too many ideas in too little time almost always follows this sentiment.

---

2. E. Tufte, *The Cognitive Style of PowerPoint* (self-published, 2003).

Instead, to convey complex information in a structure that people can mentally manage, add those stopping points. The group can use them to review, reinforce, and assess the relative importance of new concepts against what has been covered previously. Breaking things into manageable chunks of five (and reviewing at the end of each chunk) provides a structure that allows people to apply context on their own.

Doing Agenda Math

Dave could have built a better agenda by using math. Keep in mind the scale of an idea itself: about a sentence or two, describing a single fact or phenomenon. At a rate of 5 ideas every 10 minutes, Dave could have covered 30 ideas in an hour. To allow people time for review to build better, more actionable memories, cut that number in half, down to about 15, and do allow for those review breaks every other 10 minutes. Dave allocated as much time for discussion and review as he did for presentation. In one hour, he covered 5 complex ideas for 10 minutes each, and then discussed and applied them for another 10 minutes, three times (see Figure 3.4). This rate can establish a good baseline pace for any presentation.

FIGURE 3.4 Five just-complex-enough ideas every 10 minutes, followed by another 10 minutes for review.

> **DAVE'S *ORIGINAL* DESIGN PRINCIPLE AGENDA**
> - Review a principle (8 minutes).
> - Discuss a principle (2 minutes).
> - (Repeat six times.)
>
> ――――――――――――
>
> **DAVE'S *ADJUSTED* DESIGN PRINCIPLE AGENDA**
> - Review all six principles (10 minutes).
> - Five applications of a single principle (10 minutes).
> - Discuss applications of a single principle (10 minutes).
> - Five applications of a second principle (10 minutes).
> - Discuss applications of a second principle (10 minutes).

Despite this being an improvement, there is a problem that could still send this meeting off the rails. When attendees talk to each other, the conversation gets messy in larger groups because you have tangents. But tangents can be managed by applying the content to scale against the number of people in the room. Sound confusing? Let's simplify.

Ideas Move Among People Better in Groups

Tangents always happen in group conversations. Tangents aren't inherently good or bad; it's just the brain attempting to find meaning. You look for a pattern that you can use to make decisions that seem logical. In meetings, pattern recognition presents a challenge because each person's pursuit of a pattern can lead them in a different direction.

Getting the resulting mess of unpredictable tangents to a productive outcome feels like herding cats. You become the conversation police by putting boundaries on easily distracted, wandering minds. More effective than policing, however, is scaling discussion into smaller groups.

With structured small groups, people end up regulating their own tangents without you needing to monitor everything that's being said.

> *How people sit affects how they relate. For example, to get small groups working together, put them in a circle. To get a large group of people talking in a unified conversation, make sure that the group is on either side of a long table facing each other.*
>
> **—KATE RUTTER**
> **FOUNDER AND STRATEGIC SKETCHER, INTELLETO**

One of the largest meetings I've ever facilitated was for the United States Holocaust Memorial Museum staff of the Smithsonian Institution. We had a large room filled with more than 50 people. All were invested in improving the museum patron experience—helping them learn more about the museum's exhibits and connect with the museum's content—in a deeply personal way.

Remember the points of the agreement diagram explaining 66 points between 12 different people? Here's what that looks like for 50 people—it includes 1,225 points of agreement (see Figure 3.5). It seems unfathomable to get that many different people on the same page. But the meeting I facilitated didn't have that intention. Instead, we intended to have everyone follow a similar, structured journey through a set of ideas. Ending up in different places was part of the intent of the meeting.

> *The six and 90 rule is a great place to start planning any meeting. Conversations won't get sufficiently deep with more than six people, and conversations run out of gas after about 90 minutes.*
>
> **—JAMES MACANUFO**
> **CREATIVE DIRECTOR, PIXEL PRESS AND COAUTHOR, GAMESTORMING**

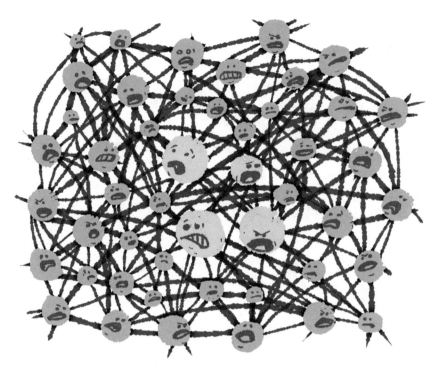

FIGURE 3.5 How many points of agreement are there between 50 people in a meeting? Let's say "a bunch."

If there were just 12 people in the room, we *could* have pursued that large number of 66 points of agreement. Imagine that each of those points of agreement is a complex idea that needs to be put into groups of five at a time. Here's another way to do your agenda math.

1. Divide 66 just-complex-enough concepts by 5 for 13 groups of concepts.

2. Multiply 13 groups by 20 minutes, which allows 10 minutes for presentation followed by 10 minutes for discussion for a rough estimate of the total number of minutes. That's a total of 260 minutes, or four and a half hours.

3. This doesn't include any time for going on tangents and getting creative. Add time for that.

4. Weep—and then buy a lot of energy bars.

What if instead of a 12-person, all-hands discussion, you break into two groups of six, seated together? (See Figure 3.6.) For six people to reach an understanding, there are 15 points of agreement. That will take 60 minutes using the above math. Roughly estimate 15 minutes for getting creative at the conclusion, and 15 minutes for transitions, and you end up with 90 minutes, which fits nicely into the six and 90 rule James mentioned earlier.

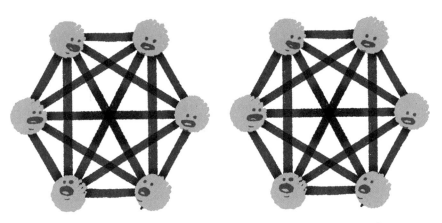

FIGURE 3.6 Two six-person groups of people can cover the same amount of content in about half as much time as one group of twelve can.

Each of those smaller groups can manifest the outcome of their discussion as a single conclusion, represented in a just-complex-enough concept. If each of the two groups presents a single idea, you've got only one point of agreement left: one group of six aligning with the other group of six. If you spend another 15 minutes exploring the differences and consolidating ideas between the two groups, the total time is still under two hours. That's less than half of the four plus hours.

Breaking into groups during meetings redistributes the cognitive load of understanding, especially when you have more than seven people in a meeting. If you've got eight, break into two groups of four. Got 15? Do three groups of five. This pattern easily scales into large group workshops, such as the one I facilitated for the Holocaust

Museum. We had seven groups of up-to-seven people thinking through specific digital exhibition strategies. After two hours, we had come to agreement, as a group of 50(!), about three unique, viable approaches to solving a complex problem.

In big meetings, working in smaller groups saves you time, money, and human costs.

The Cost of Meetings

The simplest way to calculate the cost of a meeting is by multiplying the hourly wage of all attendees against the time allotted. Here's an example: a reasonable hourly wage for a plumber in 2016 was $25 an hour.[3] What if when you hired a plumber to install a new faucet, the plumber had to meet with three other plumbers for one hour to plan the solution? What might have been two hours of labor for a cost of $50 now becomes a $100 meeting (four people multiplied by one hour, multiplied by $25 per hour). The cost of the work, including the meeting, has tripled (see Figure 3.7). Design agency billable rates are easily more than $200 per hour. Lawyers bill at $1,000 per hour, and they have *plenty* of meetings. Think about a successful modern company of more than 50,000 people, which pays its employees well. The term "staggering" doesn't begin to describe the expense.

But human costs should be considered in addition to hourly costs. People are less effective at completing their jobs when they transition in and out of meetings. They interrupt a state of flow: the state where working becomes as engaging and productive as possible.

Assume that to be minimally effective in any job, you need six hours of focused working time (or more) alone each week. It should be relatively

3. "Careers," *US News and World Report*, http://money.usnews.com/careers/best-jobs/plumber/salary

easy to find only six hours between Monday and Friday. But meetings turn workdays into a Swiss cheese network of transitions from one thing to the next. Six hours of uninterrupted time can be tough to find on a busy calendar, and even harder to protect.

FIGURE 3.7 How much would it cost if plumbers needed to meet about plumbing, before plumbing?

Giving Dave a Less Brittle Agenda

Dave lost control of his design principles presentation when two senior folks realized they had different expectations of the meeting's outcome. His meeting had eight attendees including himself, and he was trying to cover about 12 concepts, consisting of six design principles and one detailed example of each.

Ahead of time, Dave could have done the math like this.

1. Eight people will require 28 points of agreement for *each* of his six ideas, totaling 168 unique concepts that needed to be bounced around between all attendees.

2. 168 concepts will take about 11 hours to cover at a reasonable scale of 10 minutes for five ideas and 10 minutes to review.

It's no wonder that he only got through two or three principles, even with the CEO derailing.

Here's one way in which Dave could have revised his agenda, that accommodates for more content in less time using the approaches you've seen.

DAVE'S FINAL ADJUSTED DESIGN PRINCIPLE AGENDA

- Review all six principles (10 minutes).
- Discuss all six principles (10 minutes).
- Divide the group into two subgroups: a design group (design team, Group 1) and a business outcomes group (leadership, Group 2).
- Group 1: Review five to seven design applications of a single principle (10 minutes).
- Group 1: Discuss design applications of single principle (10 minutes).
- Group 2: Review five to seven business outcomes of a single principle (10 minutes).
- Group 2: Discuss applications of single principle (10 minutes).
- Reconvene the larger group and share key discussion points from each subgroup (20 minutes).

There are other ways Dave could have prepared a less brittle agenda that accomplished the same goals. He could have reset the meeting at the first sign of trouble by having everyone pair up to reduce complexity and increase speed. Each pair could explore two design principles in 10 minutes, developing their own ideas of how they could be applied to the existing collection of websites and products. After 10 minutes, everyone would share their two principles and how they discussed or applied them.

A DIFFERENT ADJUSTED DESIGN PRINCIPLE AGENDA

- Review all six principles (10 minutes).
- Discuss all six principles (10 minutes).
- Create working pairs.
- Working pairs (three pairs) discuss and apply design principle 1 (10 minutes).
- Working pairs (three pairs) discuss and apply design principle 2 (10 minutes).
- Reconvene the larger group and share key discussion points from each pair (20 minutes).

This might take some additional time, because Dave would be critiquing along the way. One hour could get the group though six principles via this approach, however. Each person in the meeting would have been able to dive into and apply two principles (as well as participate in a final discussion about the other four). Scaling people and ideas in different ways over the same amount of time would have helped Dave reach his intended outcome, but with more flexibility to account for the unpredictable nature of meetings.

WHAT YOU NEED TO KNOW

You can design an agenda to scale well and be flexible, even if it doesn't go as expected. Here are some steps to make a flexible agenda based on the number of ideas, people, and minutes you have in mind.

Start with the content. Establish a target cadence for the topics being introduced. Take the number of just-complex-enough topics or concepts you hope to cover and divide that number by five. The resulting number is the amount of 20-minute "content sections" of time you should allot.

Each section provides 10 minutes to present each set of five ideas, followed by some breathing room for application of the ideas for another 10 minutes. In an hour, you can explore about 15 ideas, but you're probably better off doing a little less than that to allow time for tangents and some creative exploration.

Example: For seven people or fewer:

- One "content section" = 10 minutes of presentation + 10 minutes of reflection and discussion

- 15 different ideas divided by 5 = 3 content sections

- 20 minutes per section times 3 content sections = 60 minutes

Adjust the agenda for the desired number of people or the constraint of time. Do you need to add more content or more people into the discussion? Are the topics you meant to cover giving birth to unexpected, but legitimate, additional topics?

Improve your use of time by breaking into groups to scale into smaller, parallel discussions. Include time at the end for each smaller group to "share out" to the larger group to consolidate the original goals.

Example: For larger groups (let's say 15):

- Break into enough groups to achieve an equal distribution of people in groups that are no smaller than five, but no larger than seven. For 15 people, that would be three groups.

- Cover the intended ideas at the cadence established by the previous formula (around 60 minutes for 15 concepts).

- Add 5 to 10 minutes for each group at the end of the small group to present their ideas (another 30 minutes for each group).

4

Manage Conflict
with Facilitation

I t's 2012, and Dawn was working as the director of a regional
news website that served millions of people across three
different states in the Northeast United States. She was
dealing with a big change in her industry that was creating
conflicts in her meetings. While it was too expensive to
undergo another redesign of the website, a redesign was
necessary to stay relevant in a changing market—a market
that was migrating rapidly to mobile devices. This redesign
also had to happen in the context of decreasing advertising
revenues, because fewer people were visiting their mobile-
unfriendly site. She was in the awkward position of having to
argue for investing in something that, month to month, was
producing less income.

During the previous redesign, Dawn's team did not build the website to look good on smartphones. But by 2012, nearly one-third of its site traffic was from those types of devices, and that percentage was steadily rising—and unfortunately, abandoning the site almost immediately. She knew that she needed to pursue a responsive design, which would provide readers with a website that reformatted itself to display properly on any size screen.

Dawn had convened the meeting with senior leadership to talk about mobile strategy. She posited that responsive design would challenge their conventional understanding of design, in that when something had been "designed," it would look the same no matter what the circumstances were. This made it difficult to discuss in groups where not everyone had the same understanding of how to design one thing that would appear differently across multiple contexts.

Dawn began with a demonstration of the *Boston Globe* website, one of the first large news sites to go responsive. While she walked through how the *Globe* website functioned on different size screens, she encountered the usual questions about responsive design.

"So, will it look this small on a desktop?"

"Why are the ads so small?"

"Will people really scroll that much to read an article?"

But then a question that really mattered came from Dawn's supervisor.

"Am I to understand that we'll have to rebuild our site from scratch and abandon all of the code that we've just had our team build?"

Dawn confirmed that this was the case and added, "If we don't do this now, in the short term, we'll lose readers as people abandon our website because it doesn't work on the devices they use. This will decrease our advertising income. But more importantly, we won't be able to adapt our website as devices evolve in the long term. The next device will always be different, but this approach ensures that our content will format itself legibly, regardless of what devices people are using."

The CEO replied, "We simply don't have the budget to rebuild our entire website right now."

Conflict Is Not a Bad Word

A meeting is a tool. Like any other tool, meetings can be well designed or poorly designed, based on how well they achieve intended outcomes while managing constraints. Constraints so far have included the core elements of meetings: people (and their brains), ideas, and time. Conflicts that exist between team members, business goals, and other competing concerns are added constraints that merit a more in-depth look.

Sometimes, you avoid conflict at work because it is emotionally challenging and creates discomfort. When there is a difference between two people's versions of success, no one likes the feeling of losing or being wrong. But without addressing, exploring, and resolving conflict, work doesn't get done. Ignoring a standing conflict leads to the same problems popping up in your work repeatedly.

> *Someone who anticipates conflict in meetings is the most likely person to initiate the conflict which they expect.*
>
> —ADAM CONNOR
> VP ORGANIZATIONAL DESIGN AND TRAINING, MAD*POW AND
> COAUTHOR, *DISCUSSING DESIGN*

Conflict can also be a natural part of the work itself. For example, a consultant's goals and a client's goals are in some ways opposing. Clients want to maximize investment in a service by spending as little as possible. They spend limited resources on a project or resource that they hope will improve their viability in a competitive market, like a new website.

Consultants do their best work, however, when timelines are flexible enough to accommodate surprises and resources are healthy enough to support better decisions based on research and observations. This requires as many resources as a client is willing to spare.

This natural, client-consultant conflict appears in project pitches, competitive bidding question-and-answer sessions, and scope-creep arguments. However, these meetings are essential to both parties. When meetings like these are well-executed, it defines and depersonalizes the conflict. These conversations are best positioned to navigate a conflict between limited resources and lofty goals toward a positive outcome.

Even though conflict shouldn't be feared or avoided, it does need to be managed (see Figure 4.1). When managed effectively, conflict supports a group's ability to make a good decision. The best tool to help a group make good decisions while still giving complex conflicts the respect they deserve is facilitation. Facilitation is a deceptively familiar word, because it sounds like something you know, but means different things in different workplaces. For the purposes of designing better meetings for your job, our definition of facilitation consists of two things.

- Facilitation is an explicitly designated role for managing conflict. That role is filled by a single individual, or multiple individuals when you have multiple small groups, with each group having its own facilitator.

- Facilitators create a productive pattern of conversation, built on divergence and convergence. This pattern encourages tangents, but also manages tangents to direct the conversation toward decisions.

FIGURE 4.1 Conflict is uncomfortable but necessary. Without facilitation, it isn't manageable.

Facilitation as a Role

In theory, meeting facilitation requires two simple steps. First, a facilitator presents a structure that the discussion will follow, usually known as the *meeting agenda*. Second, the facilitator guides participants through that agenda, keeping everyone on task with minimum interference. In practice, getting those two things to happen isn't simple—it requires a skilled facilitator, as well as a culture that supports the facilitator's success. Facilitation works exceptionally well when it's clear what jobs the facilitator will and won't do, and what jobs attendees will do in service of having a better meeting experience.

The most enduring job description of a facilitator is found within Doyle and Strauss' *How to Make Meetings Work*.[1] Their book defines facilitation as one of four roles that must be occupied to make meetings work. Those roles include the facilitator of the meeting, the recorder of the meeting, the leader who needs the meeting, and the attendee(s) (see Figure 4.2). The most common mistakes a facilitator can make usually result from not following Doyle and Strauss' simple guidelines for these roles.

Capture

Contributor

Facilitator

Intent/Leader

FIGURE 4.2 Four roles that make meeting facilitation work, from Doyle and Strauss.

Common Mistakes That Facilitators Make

The obvious part of the role of facilitators occurs during the meeting: they manage the process and coordinate discussion. They pay attention to who is speaking and assess how well the conversation is reaching its intended goal, as it takes place. They adjust the agenda as necessary by

1. Michael Doyle and David Strauss, *How to Make Meetings Work* (New York: Berkeley Publishing Group, 1993, original edition, 1976).

managing who speaks, limiting how long they speak, or providing ways to make contributions other than speaking.

Facilitators frequently fail in two ways. The first happens before the meeting has started. A facilitator should collaborate with stakeholders (dubbed "leaders" by Doyle and Strauss) to determine the best structure for a discussion, rather than arbitrarily decide on their own. The best structure will produce a desired outcome: final decisions, better understanding of a problem, or whatever form the outcome is supposed to take. That outcome should be heavily informed, if not completely defined, by stakeholders in the organization.

The second way facilitators fail is when they forget to stay neutral. Dawn's meeting to advocate for a responsive design budget was flawed in this fashion. She was clearly invested in the outcome. A facilitator should pose questions to stimulate discussion, instruct participants of desired behaviors, and answer questions that come up about what to do next. The facilitator is a balancing force, keeping contributions equal and fair. It's tempting, but dangerous and sometimes ineffective, to turn passion for a topic into a desire to facilitate a discussion around that topic. It's difficult to stay neutral about something you care about deeply. However, when the group detects bias, they can no longer trust your facilitation.

Common Mistakes That Prevent Facilitation

Doyle and Strauss describe three additional roles surrounding the facilitator, which make their job more likely to succeed. The first is a public recorder who should be focused on real-time capture of the discussion. The second is a group member who should be focused on contributions. (Group members comprise most of the people in a meeting larger than five or so.) The last is a leader (the stakeholder) who has stated the intent of the meeting for all involved, ideally before the meeting ever begins.

There are several pitfalls associated with those additional roles. For example, the public recorder is often mistaken for the scribe mentioned in Chapter 2, "The Design Constraint of All Meetings," but that person's job is not a transcription of everything people say. A recorder captures key concepts during a discussion in a publicly visible way in real time. If the recorder is doing this on a wall or a whiteboard, writing down everything everyone says is impossible. Recording in this reduced, public fashion—handwritten or hand-drawn, large, and visually accessible by the group—creates a support system for listening. If people miss something with their ears, they can look up with their eyes and recall it. It offloads individual memory into what the authors call "group memory."[2] A scribe's notes on a laptop, visible only to one person, don't accomplish this. Furthermore, writing down everything everyone says won't help either. A recorder, working with a facilitator, should exercise enough judgment to know when something is worth writing and when it isn't.

Group members also forget to rely on the recorder and the facilitator. Group members should request revisions when the recorder's capture doesn't correctly reflect their perspective. They also should be monitoring the facilitation effort for perceived bias in the agenda, in the facilitator's content, or in the facilitation style.

In addition, leaders or stakeholders are often confused with facilitators. A leader is a stakeholder who is accountable for the meeting's outcome, but not necessarily for the meeting experience itself. Stakeholders should articulate those outcomes to a facilitator, who is the best-qualified person to build the right meeting experience to deliver those outcomes.

The last common error that leaders and stakeholders make is attending meetings when they shouldn't. It's fine if someone in a leadership position doesn't attend a meeting that they themselves called; it can be better when they aren't present. There's less pressure in the room—for example, attendees won't feel evaluated and therefore they will take more risks.

2. Michael Doyle and David Strauss, *How to Make Meetings Work* (New York: Berkeley Publishing Group, 1993, original edition, 1976) p. 38.

In Dawn's meeting, the presence of key stakeholders made the meeting less about the outcome of understanding responsive design and more about paying for it. If leaders or stakeholders must attend a meeting, it helps if they recast themselves as group members, sometimes holding off on major decisions until the discussion has followed a productive pattern. Being a group member is almost like not attending at all. Being "one of the team" should reduce the feeling that the discussion (and the employee) is being evaluated. A gathering that feels less hierarchical empowers group members to confront conflicts they might otherwise avoid.

Experiment with Facilitation

This system of roles, built around facilitation at its center, serves as a base layer on which any meeting can be run more efficiently. But it isn't perfect, and it requires flexibility. For example, large groups often require more than one facilitator, and small groups might support combining roles—say, combining facilitation and recording into a single job when fewer people are present.

Avoiding common mistakes will make it easier to acknowledge conflict and seek out innovative resolutions. First, start by designating a facilitator. Give someone the blessing to assess if the conversation is on track and where that track should end up. Explicitly naming a facilitator is a small change that makes a big difference. State who the facilitator is going to be at the onset of each meeting, and watch awkward silences and weird tangents start to disappear.

Dawn's meeting described at the beginning of this chapter suffered from the lack of a designated facilitator. Dawn was invested in an outcome that conflicted with her senior leadership's desire to be frugal in solving problems. She was leading the meeting from a biased position—a third-party facilitator would have been better.

If that wasn't possible, then Dawn could have facilitated, but she should have added a subject matter expert on responsive design from her team to the conversation. This additional attendee could have addressed questions as they arose, freeing Dawn to focus on the conversation itself. Dawn could have assessed where the largest gaps in their understanding of the problem existed and zeroed in on the biggest points of conflict to move the meeting toward a better strategy.

How to Record and Facilitate in Remote Meetings

Remote meetings are now common enough that for some people, it's the only kind of meeting they know. Meetings with a distributed attendance have a unique impact on two roles: the facilitator and the recorder. These jobs are different than the way they would be if everyone were in the same room.

Recording Remote Meetings

The recorder benefits from this change in that they have a host of new tools at their disposal to keep everyone looking at the same group memory. There are cloud-based documents that multiple parties can update in real time, as well as shared screen whiteboarding and sketching software. These tools allow you to broadcast group memory directly to everyone's screen while you're talking.

However, a remote recorder can't force people to pay attention to a shared screen. From time to time, the remote recorder should check in with everyone, saying, "Are these the ideas we've covered so far? Does this accurately reflect the decisions we've made?" You should allow the person doing remote capture to have a few minutes near the end of the meeting to review what has been discussed or decided, point-by-point.

Facilitating Remote Meetings

Facilitating remote meetings can be challenging. Facilitation is built on the trust of the room, and much of that trust is earned via nonverbal communication. Matching tone-of-voice, volume, vocabulary, and body positioning contribute to trust in the facilitator. In a remote meeting, you're left with only voice, and if technology is willing, a two-dimensional video. When facilitating a remote conversation, it can help to establish more ground rules regarding how to speak. For example, you might have people announce their names before they speak in the beginning of a call, until or unless everyone can tell each person apart by some other means.

Digital conference call tools (online conference calls, free video calls, and the like) can help by highlighting the name of the person speaking, and some will even track the percentage of the overall time each person speaks. This is an important point, especially as you think about your own facilitation style. Do you talk too much or not enough? Awareness of your own facilitation style, and the fit of that style to the meeting, is important. There's more on that in the next chapter.

Finally, there are remote whiteboard or sketchboard tools that enable groups of people to make contributions to public memory in real time (see Figure 4.3). Technology, however, is not always going to be consistent for everyone. If you are collaboratively sketching ideas, some may be able to draw using a mouse or a smart pen–type tool or tablet, while others may not. If you've got webcams working, you can always have everyone sketch in their own spaces using a thick line, black marker and paper, or 3 x 5 cards. The cards are better to hold up to the camera without flopping over. No matter how bad the video connection, thick, black-line sketches on a white background will always be clear.

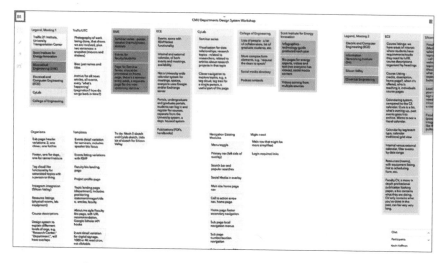

FIGURE 4.3 Capture in remote meetings can be digital and visual. Here's an example, using online collaborative whiteboarding software, called *Boardthing*, being used in real time during a meeting.

Facilitate the Pattern of Conversation

Meetings should help identify decisions that must be made, as well as help a group make those decisions together. In *Facilitator's Guide to Participatory Decision-Making,* Sam Kaner and coauthors put forth a useful pattern for thinking about how groups make decisions. The pattern illustrates an increase and decrease of the quantity of ideas a group explores over time.[3] It's superb for reflecting on how a facilitator supports a group in finding the most productive tangents in a discussion.

There are two kinds of thinking required to take advantage of tangents without wasting time. The first is divergent thinking, where you are

3. Sam Kaner, Lenny Lind, Catherine Toldi, Sarah Fisk, and Duane Berger, *The Facilitator's Guide to Participatory Decision-Making* (San Francisco: John Wiley & Sons, 2007).

increasing the *diversity* and the *quantity* of ideas you explore in a meeting. The second is convergent thinking, where you are increasing the *quality* of ideas by prioritizing the best of those ideas and reducing the quantity. If you had some leaders attending your meeting, it might look like Figure 4.4.

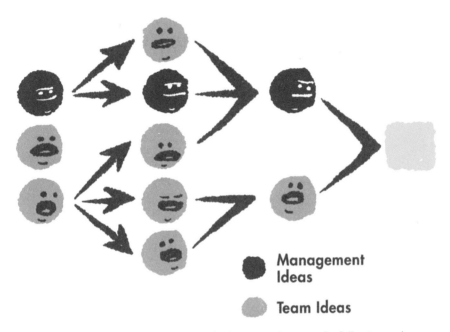

FIGURE 4.4 Divergent and convergent thinking provide a map for following and eliminating tangents in a discussion.

Following a pattern that leads with divergent thinking and concludes with convergent thinking helps you manage those tangents. Tangents can feel frustrating, but good tangents are one of the best things that come out of meetings. Good, novel ideas come from diverse opinions and experience. Going off on tangents is a way to get to those ideas. They won't all be great ideas, but a few of them could be better than what you might come up with working alone.

How to Facilitate Tangents

A good facilitator will assess and manage tangential ideas. The facilitator roughly counts the concepts being shared by tracking the discussion and decides when there are enough tangents to move on by evaluating the quality of these ideas. The facilitator helps the group "turn the corner" by declaring a point in the meeting when it's time to collect tangents and transform them into a direction or decision.

While facilitating divergent thinking, remind people to be open-minded. Divergent activities include making lists, having open-ended discussion, and collecting perspectives. During divergent thinking, it's the facilitator's job to remind the group to suspend judgment. It's OK to allow discomfort in the group and have conflict that goes unresolved. Ideas may contradict each other, but the more ideas, the better. Get the obvious ideas out of the way and move onto the ones that require a little more effort.

At some point, the facilitator should turn the boat around and switch the focus to convergence. The facilitator should help the group decide if one tangent is better than another. Where divergent thinking is about being OK with disagreement, convergent thinking is about eliminating excess, or the least likely stuff to succeed. Once the corner has been turned, the facilitator helps the group summarize the essence of each approach to decide what's worth keeping and how to act upon it.

Build the Pattern into Agendas

The facilitator should assemble agendas that open with divergent activities and close with convergent ones. A meeting that only consists of divergence is the cliché of unproductive brainstorming. Making a list of what could be possible is only worth doing if the group will also be held accountable for making some sense out of their list before they leave.

Many people criticize brainstorming as a waste of time.[4] Meetings that build a list of ideas without refining that list into actionable choices are divergence without convergence, and won't help you much.

Doing convergent first is no better. Leading with convergent thinking prevents the group from making new suggestions that you may need. Starting with an explicit goal of "eliminating options" feels frustrating because there's no chance to explore what might have been some good ideas. People tune out when there's no room to add anything, and they retreat to checking in on laptops and phones. People are blamed for not paying attention, but tuning out can be a symptom of an ill-considered conversation pattern.

Using a conversational pattern to surface conflicts in process, capabilities, and expectations is one of the best outcomes of good facilitation. It's a direct route to the heart of a problem. A facilitator shines a light on the competing perspectives that can lead to shared clarity. It feels intense, but at the same time it is productive. That intensity can sometimes come from a fear of change, and that fear creates discomfort. It's like when you're asked to think outside the box, but as soon as you do, the team, or your leadership, resists. Sarah B. Nelson shows you how you can facilitate that discomfort toward better outcomes.

4. Tomas Chamorro-Premuzic, "Why Group Brainstorming Is a Waste of Time," *Harvard Business Review*, March 2015, https://hbr.org/2015/03/why-group-brainstorming-is-a-waste-of-time

HOW DO YOU MANAGE THE CONFLICT BETWEEN INNOVATIVE THINKING AND A NATURAL FEAR OF CHANGE?

Sarah B. Nelson
Design Studio Manager, IBM
Founder, Radically Human

Sarah B. Nelson helps creative leaders develop thriving teams, so they can focus on designing inspired products and services. Her super power: turning a frustrated group of coworkers into a creative group of colleagues. Her quest: uncover the secret to repeatable, high-quality collaboration.

A stakeholder loudly proclaims that she wants innovative new ideas only to reject them out of hand. Sound familiar? You've run into the Creativity Bias. When Mueller, Melwani, and Goncalo discovered the Creativity Bias, they learned that when people reject the new and novel, it happens subconsciously.[5] Novelty sets off powerful survival alarm bells. Novel ideas imply change, change implies risk, and risk could mean expulsion from the herd, certain starvation, and imminent death. Sound dramatic? You bet.

Human beings are hardwired to protect their physical and social well-being. Once alarm bells have been sounded, the conscious mind begins to construct an argument that prevents the change from occurring. As a meeting facilitator, understanding the psychological complexity triggered by discomfort will enable you to plan for, work with, and recover from any fallout that may occur. Beyond that you can intentionally create an environment where discomfort can lead to excellent creative outcomes.

5. Jennifer S. Mueller, Shimul Melwani, and Jack A. Goncalo, "The Bias Against Creativity: Why People Desire but Reject Creative Ideas," *Psychological Science* 2010, http://digitalcommons.ilr.cornell.edu/cgi/viewcontent.cgi?article=1457&context=articles

Getting Comfortable with Discomfort

Creativity and discomfort go hand-in-hand. If your team feels comfortable, your team may not be pushing itself hard enough. Discomfort can push you to more inventive solutions or address previously unspoken issues. Pushing through discomfort into uncharted territory can open opportunities that originally seemed impossible. Years of facilitation taught me an important lesson—before you can create discomfort with a group, you need to clarify your own relationship with discomfort. I used to believe my job was protecting myself and others from discomfort. Discomfort equaled disagreement, which equaled conflict, which equaled failure.

After a lot of effort, I embraced the creative power of discomfort. A little discomfort here pays off big later. As someone facilitating meetings, you need to find your relationship to discomfort, too. Notice what happens when you encounter it. What do you think, do, say, or feel? You have a unique relationship to discomfort, and so does everyone else in the room. Some people in a meeting will enjoy creative discomfort, but others won't. As a facilitator, you'll have to work with these attitudes without losing sight of the target outcome.

Spotting Discomfort in the Wild

Spotting discomfort requires all your senses. People give off many clues about their current level of discomfort. Some will be obvious, while others will be subtler—people may check their phones, stay silent, start shooting down ideas, or even start cracking jokes.

Once you know your relationship with discomfort and what it might look like in a meeting, you are ready to lead a room full of people through what could be an edgy session.

CONTINUES ➤

CONTINUED ➤

Managing Discomfort

As a facilitator, your job is to lead them through a process, help them navigate traps, and achieve meeting outcomes. There are two simple steps that help put discomfort in a productive place:

1. Acknowledge potential discomfort and ask permission to guide them through. Say something like "You will likely feel pushed in this process, and it will make you uncomfortable. This is totally normal in any creative process. When it happens, I will guide you through it. Do I have your permission to do that?" This simple act relaxes people and builds trust in your facilitation. You've shown them where you will go, given them an idea of what it will be like, and assured them that you have their back.

2. When people start shifting in their seats, the room is suddenly dead silent, or you sense confusion or open combat, interrupt. Say something like "Fantastic! How's everyone feeling? A little uncomfortable?" Wait for reluctant nods. "Perfect! We are in the right place. What do we need to do to get past this?" Usually, these simple words are often enough to get a group back on track. If they aren't enough, take a break.

Creating Discomfort

Your next goal will be to seed discomfort purposefully. You're getting the group prepared to stretch beyond their comfort zone, so this can happen easily. Before (or sometimes during) the session, identify the elephants in the room: the touchy subjects, the unspoken taboos, and the questions no one will ask. Then find creative ways to bring them out.

Sometimes, just pointing out an uncomfortable subject can be enough. I was facilitating a process-redesign workshop for a prominent company in Silicon Valley. This company prided itself on being a flat, consensus-driven organization. Frustrating to the group, a powerful executive inserted his opinion regularly and, in doing so, turned the consensus-driven process to chaos, undermining their ability to do great work. In pre-workshop interviews, each team member shared this same frustration. But the topic disappeared once they got in the room with each other—not one person brought up the executive's behavior. As a result, the group could not come up with constructive ways to work with him.

I took a chair, one with wheels on it, wrote the executive's name on a Post-it Note and pushed the chair into the middle of the room. I asked, pointing at the chair, "How does this topic impact the process you are designing right now?" I was met with deafening silence. Discomfort? You bet. Did I push it even further? Not this time. I knew that just that act would bring the topic into the room and might allow them to approach it creatively.

As a facilitator, sometimes you can't force people to overcome their discomfort right away. But you can plant a seed that will flourish long after the meeting is over.

WHAT YOU NEED TO KNOW

It's easier to identify and manage conflicts in a meeting when a facilitator has been identified. So step one is making sure that you're designating someone to serve in the facilitation role, every meeting. Then do the following:

- Facilitate without bias—don't facilitate discussions when you have strong opinions about the outcome.

- Identify someone in each meeting to create a public recording, writing and sketching key concepts to create a visual feedback loop supporting the discussion.

You should also support the facilitator with clear meeting goals that come from or are endorsed by leadership.

Once you've identified a facilitator and established what the boundaries of their job are, they can guide the group along a conversational pattern. The best guides will watch the conversation as it diverges and help it to converge at the right time. When facilitating, do the following to support better decision-making in meetings:

- Make space for both divergence (more ideas) and convergence (fewer ideas) to exist.

- Lead agendas with divergence and conclude with convergence.

- Avoid having conversations where you only follow one of the two patterns. Divergence-only meetings are pointless brainstorming. Convergence-only meetings disenfranchise possible new, good solutions.

5

Facilitation Strategy and Style

Amira is a content strategist who specializes in helping organizations articulate their brand through the content that they publish. To simplify somewhat, she executes this process in two steps. First, she helps organizations explore how they are perceived by their customers, which she calls their "current brand." Then she helps map out aspirational brand aspects that the organization would like to build into their perception. She explores these two spaces in a workshop with her clients, and it always feels uncomfortable. It's a necessary discomfort, but it can be managed by thinking about her own facilitation strategy and style.

Amira was in a workshop facilitating a discussion of a current and aspirational brand with a well-known print magazine. This company wanted to make the transition from being perceived as a magazine company to being considered a smart digital company, with easy-to-access, timely content on the devices people kept in their pocket. It was and is a challenge common to many struggling publishing companies.

She had a simple goal for this meeting. She wanted the group to identify and agree upon four descriptive phrases in which customers perceived their brand aspects, called *pillars*.[1] The group that would accomplish this together consisted of senior editorial staff for each of the magazine sections, as well as senior editors and the editor-in-chief.

"Who people believe that we are (as a brand)" is an intimate question for employees and leadership. Anticipating conflict, she started by confronting the group with a stark statement of truth.

"Why have you failed to gain any traction in the digital market?"

Several editors immediately challenged that statement, citing successful pilots and one app based on their recipe section, which seemed to have had modest success. These feelings were openly in direct opposition to the goals of the meeting, which were expressed by senior editors, who didn't see collective, organizational success in the digital space. They only saw experiments. An argument broke out, and Amira did her best to facilitate the debate.

She scanned faces and watched body language, and could tell that people were troubled. To address their fears, she briefly targeted individuals in the room to share their concerns. After a quick scan, she abandoned those check-ins to keep the group on the agenda she had worked so hard to build.

After a tense hour, she'd gotten the group to agree on two of the four current brand pillars she was shooting for, but none of the aspirational

---

1. Based on the "Identity Pillars" exercise by Ahava Liebtag. Ahava Leibtag, *The Digital Crown: Winning at Content on the Web* (Boston: Morgan Kaufmann, 2013).

ones. Workshops on tough topics can easily get out of hand. Every group Amira had ever worked with got into similar conflicts born of looking in the mirror and not liking what they saw. This time, however, she couldn't adapt her facilitation strategy and style to be successful. Facilitation is a nuanced skill, and a good facilitator can take the temperature of the room and adjust accordingly.

In the previous chapter, we defined the role of the facilitator, an environment that supports facilitation, and a conversational pattern that helps it all succeed. But your facilitation approach should be tailored to the outcomes you seek and the type of people (and organization) seeking them. This customization can come about in two ways: building questions strategically and tweaking your style.

Asking the Right Questions

Facilitation succeeds based on good questions. A well-designed, well-timed question illuminates possibilities to a group that is stuck, or reframes a problem to a group that agrees. But there's a problem with the way facilitators usually pose questions.

Whether coming from a designated facilitator or not, questions asked in meetings are usually loaded. They live in a space I like to call "proud inquiry" as a play on Edgar Schein's concept of "humble inquiry." (I'll get to that in a moment.) A proud inquiry-style question is one where the asking party already has an answer in mind. You believe you have a solution, so you ask a question that subtly (or not so subtly) points the group in the right direction. This style of question is asked only to confirm or expand upon assumptions.

Serving a meeting without bias means eliminating the facilitator's own biases. Biased questions undermine trust in the facilitation process. An attendee will think, "Why does my answer matter, if you've already figured this out?" If you have a lot of answers in mind before a meeting starts, you are also more likely to offer to facilitate when there isn't a designated facilitator. As a result, you might see meetings as positive, because meetings produce the work that you believe is the "right work."

People leading meetings tend to think they are productive.
People invited to meetings tend to think they are not.

—ELISE KEITH
COFOUNDER, LUCID MEETINGS

That's not true facilitation. Developing facilitation questions per Edgar Schein's cultural research methodology—called "humble inquiry"— helps correct this tendency.[2] Humble inquiry is a methodology for researching the differences between the culture an organization believes it has (the espoused culture) and the actual working culture in place (what it's really like). The methodology includes an approach to asking questions that are easily adapted for use in meetings. It consists of four categories of questions to elicit specific information, including feelings, motivations, actions, and systems.

Questions That Surface Feelings

When people have strong feelings about something, it can be helpful to tackle those feelings in a straightforward way. It's the facilitator's job to assess whether tackling a specific feeling could be productive. Questions can be engineered to elicit an emotional state from the people in the room, or to explore the emotional state of audiences affected by the meeting's outcomes.

- When we discovered that during the first quarter we operated at a loss, how did everyone feel?

- When our target audience first opens our app/website, how should they feel?

- If you could solve the supply chain issues holding us up, how would you feel?

---

2. Edgar Schein, *Humble Inquiry* (San Francisco: Berrett-Kohler Publishers, 2013).

Questions That Surface Motivations

If you're concerned about too many potential tangents, questions about motivation help assess whether a tangent merits further discussion. Motivation questions reveal expected or desired outcomes, assumed outside factors, or personal guiding principles, all of which might not be shared across the group. Exploring motivations opens these topics up for better decision-making.

- What were you hoping would happen when the department budget was reduced?
- What did you think would happen when we increased our new user sign-ups by 25%?
- What were you going for with this creative direction?

Questions That Surface Actions

Sometimes, people don't provide enough detail, or they provide too much detail. Questions about intended actions help you find the right level of detail. When asking questions about the actions a team (or its members) intends to take, the amount of detail should be tied to the work itself.

If you're supporting a complicated process, like signing up and paying for a service, be more detailed in your inquiry about actions. If you're supporting something potentially fuzzy, like predicting the possible future health of a line of business, ask questions that move people the next step in a series more rapidly, with less detail.

- What would you do to build interest in our content?
- What is the first step we should take in executing this strategy?
- What does our audience do to solve this problem now without our product?

Questions That Surface Systems

Where action questions help identify the steps in a process, questions about systems address how changing a process or a system can affect the outcome. These questions focus on interdependencies between multiple factors. System questions are also good for helping facilitate agreement between people who have very different perspectives on a problem. To build good system questions, think about asking, "OK, then what's next?" or "How does one thing affect the other?"

- If we successfully identified six user stories for this application, how will we prioritize functionality?

- What needs to be accomplished in this sprint that, if unsuccessful, could hold up our next sprint?

- What are management's concerns that would impact our direction?

Using Question Design in Facilitation

Don't build facilitation questions by trying to check off each of these categories. Begin by defining the intended outcomes of your meeting. Then write the questions that you believe will help a group arrive at those outcomes, in whatever form they emerge. This approach gets a natural tendency toward proud inquiry out of your system and onto paper. Once that tendency is out in the open, remove the assumptions from your questions. Then rephrase each question so that it leans toward one of the four categories: surfacing emotions, finding motivations, defining desired behaviors, or architecting complex interactions.

Amira had a few problems with the design of questions in her meeting. First, the question she asked was filled with proud inquiry. Second, there were a few opportunities to use more strategic questions. One opportunity was in the assessment of what people believed about the current and aspirational brand. Moving people along at a brisk pace, she could have used feeling questions to get to her goals.

- (Feeling) What do your readers feel about the magazine currently? Amira could have requested answers in the form of one word or a short phrase. After collecting these answers, she could have surveyed the room to prioritize, following the divergence/convergence conversational pattern from Chapter 4, "Manage Conflict with Facilitation."
- (Action) What do you want people to do when they think about your brand?

In addition, questions can help people be more aware of their own behavioral patterns. In a daylong workshop, you cannot hope to understand all the personalities in a room. Break obvious patterns by changing the tone of the conversation with a good question, rather than being dismissive to stay on the agenda (as Amira did). It takes practice to do this skillfully. Questions might be along the lines of the following:

- (Motivation) Can you speak about why someone would do what you want them to do, from a personal experience?
- (System, in response to "We can't do this because we do business differently.") What are other repercussions of behaviors that we desire from our readers that affect how we do business?

Well-designed questions support better facilitation. Bringing those questions to life in a conversation is largely affected by personal facilitation style. Are you talkative and confrontational, or are you quiet and patient? Facilitation reflects the personal style of the facilitator. That personal style may also need to be adapted to suit the needs of a specific conflict or even the culture of the organization.

Facilitation Styles

Facilitation is a balancing act. It requires demonstrating empathy for a group's interests and capabilities while simultaneously keeping them away from tempting but unproductive lines of discussion. The effort and focus required to maintain that balance varies based on what kind of person you are and what kind of topic or group you're facilitating. These three spectrums—scripted to improvisational, drawing to speaking, and space making to space filling—are designed to help you get a better sense of your own (or anyone's) facilitation style. They will also help to assess when a style supports a meeting, or when it needs something different.

Scripted to Improvisational

Do you plan agendas so precisely that you prescribe the number of minutes per topic? Do you distribute a written discussion guide in advance? If so, then you probably facilitate more in a scripted style. Scripted facilitation is well suited for organizations where meetings tend to be frequent, aimless, and meandering. The clarity provided by a more rigid discussion guide will seem novel and be welcomed.

Scripted facilitators can come across as less flexible, or at worst, inauthentic. A script helps, but you don't want to seem like you wouldn't be able to succeed without it. When you are perceived as inauthentic, people will believe that you're more invested in seeing your plan followed than a positive outcome. If you sense any of those responses to your style, it's time to become more improvisational (see Figure 5.1).

FIGURE 5.1 Improvisational versus scripted facilitation styles.

Effective improvisational facilitators can surprise people with strong questions out of the blue, and they seem to draw from a bottomless playbook of activities. Improvisational facilitation feels challenging and requires attendees to be present and focused. When it works, it helps the group synthesize in unexpected ways.

It may seem like an improvisational facilitator is unprepared, but they are like jazz musicians. Jazz musicians seemingly pull stuff out of thin air, but it's really from tons of practice and a playbook of great ideas they've built over time. Good improvisational facilitators come prepared with a collection of conversational hacks that they can summon at will. Improvisers also convey a deep sense of empathy for the people in the room. Stopping the conversation without warning to unpack something conveys being in tune with the room's mood.

Improvisers thrive when they get rapid feedback from the conversation. That feedback helps them forecast the next question or step in the process. They struggle when people are opaque, or when they are unable to let go of the preconceived agendas. If people aren't ready or willing to let go of their expected topics, having a basic script to fall back on will keep an improviser from losing control of the room.

The meeting at the beginning of the chapter might have been better served by being more improvisational. Amira's agenda was very scripted. Since her style might be more scripted, simply having a fallback script of a few prepared challenge questions to draw from would have helped her when the discussion became too rigid. You can build a fallback script by first listing all the things that could go wrong. Then prepare a discussion question or two for each worst-case scenario.

Use improvisational planning to inject spontaneity when it's needed. Think of your script as something that you iterate upon, in real time. Be ready to say, "If this question or activity isn't working, how will I adapt?"

To hit the middle ground between scripted and improvisational, Amira could have prepared a branching agenda: a diagram of three or four steps, which outlined hypothetical discussion paths. This is like a "choose your own adventure book," and should never play out the same way twice (see Figure 5.2). Branching agendas serve groups that are ready to improvise, helping them get past the obvious to new ideas.

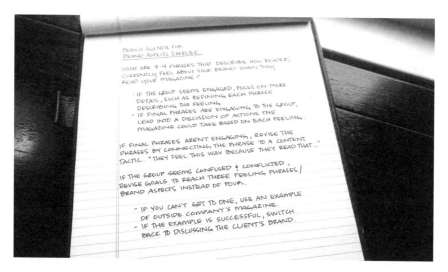

FIGURE 5.2 Branching agendas for Amira's meeting would have helped her guide improvisational choices.

Drawing to Speaking

Do you draw something to understand it clearly? Then you are more comfortable with a drawing facilitation style and might make a good visual facilitator. Visual facilitators will not move forward until they've had a chance to articulate the discussion as a sketch and then create a feedback loop of discussion around that sketch. They take advantage of the visually engaged parts of the brain discussed in Chapter 2, "The Design Constraint of All Meetings." Visuals can move a discussion to greater clarity, past the obvious into a richer understanding of a problem. It also provides a map of the discussion itself, which you can refer to if you need to explore previous ideas further.

If an organization has never been exposed to a drawing style before, it can seem "touchy feely." Visual facilitators can also be more scripted in their initial approach to starting a conversation. They might draw from a preset visual vocabulary to save time, such as Sunni Brown's,[3] or a specific framework or map, such those developed by David Sibbet.[4] The "Context Map" is an example of a visual conversation map that can be filled out. These vocabularies or frameworks don't limit the conversation at all, but they do require enough judgment to pair the right map to the conversation at hand (see Figure 5.3).

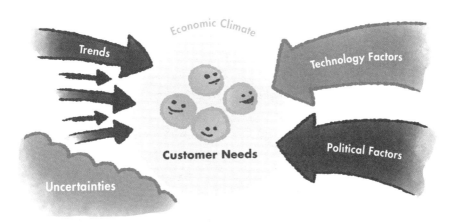

FIGURE 5.3 A context map is a good example of a visual facilitation framework, adapted from David Sibbet, founder of The Grove Consultants International.

Attendees will have varying capabilities and experience with visual thinking, and that is a challenge. You'll have to adjust the pace of reviewing the visuals to accommodate diversity. Another challenge

3. "The visual alphabet" from Sunni Brown, "The Miseducation of the Doodle," *A List Apart*, no. 322 (January 25, 2001), http://alistapart.com/article/the-miseducation-of-the-doodle
4. David Sibbet, *Visual Meetings* (Hoboken, NJ: Wiley Books, 2010), p. 84 and found at The Grove Consultants International website, https://grovetools-inc.com/collections/context-map and https://grovetools-inc.com/collections/graphic-gameplan

is the size or style of the room. Not everyone may be able to see what you've drawn. You could overcome this by getting up and moving around; however, that raises the last but most important constraint of a drawing style. This style presumes that everyone shares a similar level of visual ability. Although visuals are a powerful way to communicate, it is inherently not universally accessible. That's a great reason to balance drawing style with speaking style (see Figure 5.4).

FIGURE 5.4 Drawing versus speaking facilitation styles.

Spoken facilitation is so common that it's usually taken for granted that meetings will be run this way. Good spoken facilitation builds meaning by blending what people say with subtext picked up from their tone of voice and body language. If you are good at making people feel welcome in a conversation, you probably will facilitate in a spoken style. It comes from having a natural empathy. That empathy helps you manage multiple streams of thought (and feeling) emerging from what people say. It also helps you connect the dots between ideas, even when those connections may not be self-evident to everyone.

Spoken facilitation has built-in limits, just like visual facilitation. As you learned in Chapter 2, visuals can trigger different or greater levels of understanding. To ignore that possibility is a disservice. Spoken conversation requires an exhausting level of concentration. Some people find the volley of a good conversation energizing for a limited time. Too much talking, however, and you will miss opportunities for more considered, quiet reflection. Consider which style is most effective for you and then supplement the style you do well with the style you could do better.

If you know you lean toward spoken facilitation, find opportunities to sketch simple diagrams. Process flows like this "graphic gameplan" shown in Figure 5.5 represent an example of a way to incorporate some drawing style into your speaking.

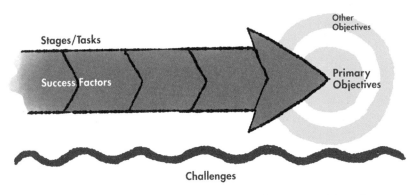

FIGURE 5.5 The Graphic Gameplan, a visual process flow approach based on action plans, adapted from David Sibbet, founder of The Grove Consultants International.

If you're better as a visual facilitator, think of your drawings as a series of images that tell a story. There will be an initial state of your sketches (before the meeting), an active state (during the meeting), and an after state (no surprise here, after the meeting). Before you begin, the halfway point, and after the sketch is completed are good times to pose questions to prompt discussion. There may be multiple halfway points; think of them as chapters in the book of your meeting. Make sure that each chapter has a title and verbally call out that title before moving on to the next sketch.

If you've never attended a meeting with a visual facilitator, try doing it a little yourself. It can be a humbling experience requiring intense concentration. But it has provided tremendous value for companies like Zappos, Disney, and TED, to name just a few. If you are wondering how to get started with visual note-taking and facilitation, Kate Rutter, an accomplished visual facilitator, shows you the way by sharing her journey toward a more meaningful way of creating meaning from meetings.

HOW CAN YOU GET STARTED WITH VISUAL FACILITATION?

Kate Rutter
Founder and Strategic Sketcher, Intelleto

Kate is an expert in visual thinking, graphic recording and facilitation, and sketchnoting and teaching. She practices all of these skills at her company, Intelleto. Previously, she led the UX teaching practice at Tradecraft, cofounded LUXr, and worked as one of the first experience designers at Adaptive Path.

Very early in my career, I was a technology director for a non-profit organization. As part of that role, I served on the executive strategic team that led an effort to revitalize our vision and mission. Our team brought in a facilitation group called *The Grove Consultants International*, led by David Sibbet. They provided a visual facilitator for us to work with. I didn't stay with that job long enough to see the process come to fruition, but I saw that visually articulating complex, abstract ideas is fundamental to groups really understanding each other in a discussion and making a discussion actionable.

I had been making pictures of ideas throughout my career: diagrams, doodles, and observational sketches. I'd never seen it applied toward the hard work of humans working together and that was just a breakthrough moment for me.

Ten years later, I was working in a user-experience design consultancy called *Adaptive Path*. All our work with digital product design happened within the machine, the laptop. We were almost always working within digital tools like Photoshop or Keynote as ways to get ideas about product interface out of our heads and into a buildable concept.

Our work became more strategic as companies started making more strategic decisions about their digital products, but we didn't have a way to share things outside the machine. We could project visuals, but we needed a way to have more abstract conversations. Without a visual facilitation practice, we were trying to cover a lot of complex information and losing each other in the process.

We developed quick, tangible tools for visual discussion. In 2007, we started to use sharpies, white paper, and sticky notes to collaborate with client groups. This cocreation approach became fundamental to our work, and also a huge selling point because people who hired us could cocreate with us. Clients could get their ideas heard in a way that many other consulting organizations just didn't know how to do.

Simple visual marks that can show someone a picture of a potential future is incredibly helpful and powerful, more so than tools like PowerPoint, spoken words, and data visualizations (Figure 5.6). Taking a lot of words and making them into a set of pictures helps people understand and grasp complexity in a much more time-effective way, which is great when you are in a meeting and time is of the essence.

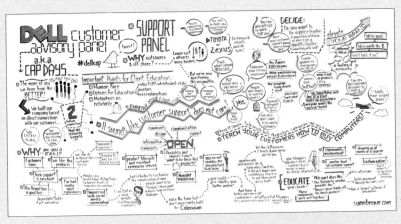

FIGURE 5.6 The results of visually facilitating a complex meeting, by Sunni Brown.

Why Visual Facilitation Works

Visual facilitation is effective in meetings for three reasons. First, our brains are highly optimized for spatial information. For example, if you imagine yourself standing in the front doorway of your childhood home, point to where the forks were kept. I don't care how old you are, you'll be able to point your hand in that direction. We have an extraordinarily powerful ancient brain system that helps us understand and remember space.

CONTINUES ➤

CONTINUED ➤

Long-form narrative writing and verbal discussions don't have that power. These are sequential forms of communication that aren't spatial. When people don't have to read something, or hear it in a sequence, spatial thinking helps people tap into that ability of their brain to see the big picture.

Second, verbal and written communication both have extraordinary richness with endless subtlety and variety. When you are forced to visualize ideas, you get rid of a lot of that detail. It forces you to identify the key messages and why they matter. What belongs near each other? What things are similar, and what is more important in a hierarchy? To put key ideas down visually, you should do that synthesis and analysis. That's why it bubbles up the big ideas. You don't have time to write down everything.

Finally, people are enchanted with hand-styled visual depictions of things. Dan Roam, the author of *Back of the Napkin*, says, "The more human the picture, the more human the response." If you showed someone a very polished, high-fidelity precise visual, it might feel like something that only a professional could do. But if you showed someone a quick sketch of the human form, with a little bit of a layout: where they're standing, what is happening around them, and the expression of emotion on that person's face, that feels accessible. It doesn't alienate.

Why Visual Facilitation Isn't Everywhere (Yet)

When people can communicate and discuss ideas with visuals, it's a very emotionally sophisticated working style. That may be why a lot of companies balk at this type of facilitation. If the unspoken social contract between employees isn't supportive of being human with each other, this technique is not going to do well in meetings. Sadly, work meetings can be one of the least human places to be doing business.

Forcing imagery out of a group with visual facilitation puts them into this place of feeling vulnerable. That creates a different sense of understanding in meetings. If you want your meetings to be human, use human techniques. Making pictures of the future is one of the most fundamentally human techniques that is out there.

Blending drawing and speaking styles would have enabled Amira to slow her brand workshop down when it inevitably reached natural conflict. A good example of blended spoken and visual facilitation is an activity called "Cover Story" from the book *Gamestorming*.[5] For a detailed agenda read *Gamestorming*, but the overall approach would work like this: Amira first spends time at the beginning of the meeting defining what success looks like visually, as the cover of a popular magazine about her type of work. What stories would be on the cover or what photograph? By phrasing success using stakeholders' brand aspects in that sketch, Amira could connect the brand identity work to the outcomes that leadership needed.

Space Making to Space Filling

The last style spectrum covers how much content you fit into the time allotted. Are you fine with pauses in the conversation? If you are, you make space. Space makers recognize that conversation takes on a life of its own, so they provide room for that conversation to go in its natural direction. They give people time to reflect on what has been covered so far. Add a few minutes at regular intervals to reflect, provide short breaks to observe the public notes, and build in periods of time where everyone circles back to a previously explored idea.

Conversations facilitated in a space-making style feel sparse but still productive. Space making is best when there is a goal of taking something further, like developing new options. Space-making facilitation is good for developing a thorough list, such as pros and cons of a decision.

Space makers aren't going to be successful with people who think aloud, using speech to process their ideas. When part of the group works this way, their pace will expand to fill spaces and dictate the conversation's rhythm. A space maker may feel like they are losing control of the meeting to a stronger personality. If you are a space maker but

5. Dave Gray, Sunni Brown, and James Macanufo, *Gamestorming* (Sebastopol, CA: O'Reilly 2010), p. 87.

are having that feeling, it's a good opportunity to switch gears into a space-filling style (see Figure 5.7).

FIGURE 5.7 Space-making versus space-filling facilitation styles.

Space fillers get antsy if there's too long of a pause. Extended silence feels like a problem. They verbalize more to maintain group focus and may have little tolerance for surprise tangents and inefficiencies. This style feels dense and can move from topic to topic quickly. Space-filling facilitation moves a conversation toward detail, refinement, and shared clarity. It's a good style for prioritization and making decisions.

Without good alignment on goals and critical concepts at the start of a meeting, space filling fails. When people aren't working from the same concepts, they need more time to suss out differences in understanding. That requires creating space, and if you are naturally a space filler, you'll have to force yourself to stop and occasionally shut up. If you give the group more time to respond, that second answer or follow-up conversation will move past the most obvious answer into more interesting or challenging spaces. Something better may be just across the horizon of an uncomfortable silence. Provide space to move through that silence.

Amira's own discomfort with people's reactions interfered with her ability to make space to explore conflicting viewpoints. You can see this in her poor question design. When challenged, Amira should have stopped taking up space and unpacked the conflict with a system question.

"Are successful experiments in the digital space the rule or the exception?" This would have helped the group align on the current state of the brand.

You should work through difficult points in a conversation by being aware of your facilitation style first and then modulating it along these three spectrums as needed. A space-filling facilitator working with a group of people locked in a conflict might need to make space to identify points of difference. Or, if you are stuck too far down into the weeds, stop talking and start drawing. When you improvise most of the time, consider sketching a backup script, just in case. Making an intentional decision to abandon your script and improvise is easier than realizing you need a script, but don't have it.

No matter where your facilitation styles sit, facilitating a lot of meetings will give you a better sense of your strengths and weaknesses. In most organizations, there are plenty of opportunities to facilitate meetings. You can formalize that facilitation in your organization by establishing a facilitation competency. Samantha Soma is a designer at General Electric on the digital team that established a facilitation competency for multiple design teams. This is how that came about.

Build a Facilitation Competency

Samantha Soma practices design facilitation at GE Digital, where she applies her diverse background in conflict resolution, mediation, community development, team building, and design thinking. This diverse background helps cross-functional teams frame problems, understand the people involved, and discover methods to solve them.

Samantha took a position devoted to design facilitation as part of a reorganization. As part of that process, a design center was built for the express purpose of convening meetings with customers and businesses to understand their design problems, and then craft project plans and solutions to solve those problems. They established a facilitation competency within the center as part of the company's core design competencies.

What Comprises a Facilitation Competency?

That facilitation competency is made up of two things. First, it's the ability to gather materials for success in a meeting. This includes information about the business, the background of the problem, and some current solutions—basically all the information you would want before trying to solve a problem. Second, it is knowing how to curate activities for an agenda that surfaces information to help designers understand the problem they are trying to solve. If you were having a meeting with high-level stakeholders, for example, you would be doing activities that surfaced more strategic information. A meeting with people in power plant operations would have different activities, because what you need from them is fundamentally different.

Building a toolkit of activities, which you can execute on-demand, is part of that competency. You're expected to learn who needs to be in a room, manage diverse agendas, and understand different levels of power and influence. It's about being able to manage and prioritize the contributions of different participants, based on what the problem truly needs. Sometimes what the problem needs isn't the same as what participants want.

Because managing varying influences is tough, preparation is a critical part of the competency, which Samantha calls "the meetings before the meeting." Very few people have the time, bandwidth, or ability to do the necessary prep work for good design facilitation. There is a lot of prep work that goes into making a successful meeting feel natural and not overly planned. The goal is to choreograph an experience carefully so that it doesn't *feel* choreographed.

For example, give people different colors of pens on purpose, so that you know who wrote what later. Make sure that you create smaller working groups with a good mix of skills, influence, and chemistry. You're investing a lot of time and resources in a meeting for the purposes of making what are likely critical design decisions.

Competency and Conflicts

Samantha tells her facilitators explicitly to allow conflict to happen. Within kickoff and problem framing meetings, conflict is a means of exploring creative tension. If you don't figure stuff out here, at the beginning, it's just going to manifest in other, far more destructive ways.

With the permission to be expressive comes a promise that you will keep everyone professionally safe to explore differences of opinion. People behave well when everyone else is behaving well, even if given space to be confrontational. Making a space for this dissent to happen can look like the meeting is failing, but the larger goal of an effective team developing a shared target is still there. Exploring conflict exposes everything that gets in the way of that shared target: it reveals what you need to remove.

One example of this in practice is that designers are taught to always revisit their parking lots. Parking lots consist of tangential ideas that were deemed valuable during a discussion, but not relevant. Designers never leave the meeting without making sure that each item in a parking lot is addressed and has a plan associated with it.

Many of these meetings are modeled after the Jack Welch "workout" approach to meetings.[6] A workout meeting is one in which everyone is empowered (and expected) to carry out any decisions that need to be made within that meeting. It's not a status meeting; it's not a discussion. You enter with a problem, and you exit with a plan. Without being able to effectively facilitate conflict, this type of meeting simply wouldn't be possible.

---

6. Noel Tichy and Ram Charan, "Speed, Simplicity, Self-Confidence: An Interview with Jack Welch," *Harvard Business Review*, September–October 1989, https://hbr.org/1989/09/speed-simplicity-self-confidence-an-interview-with-jack-welch

WHAT YOU NEED TO KNOW

Designing good framing or discussion questions has numerous benefits. It builds trust in the facilitator, it uncovers necessary detail and disagreement, and it removes the facilitator's own assumptions from the conversation. You can design better questions by following these three steps:

- From a list of outcomes, develop questions that point the conversation in what you believe to be the right direction, adding questions that allow for any tangents that will add value.

- Rewrite your questions to remove any assumptions.

- Reword them further to classify them along one of the four question classes identified in Schein's "humble inquiry" approach: emotion, motivation, action, or system. There's no need to cover all the categories in every meeting. Just think of these categories as useful in helping a group understand the difference between the intention of a single conversation and the intention of the larger project the conversation supports.

Armed with well-designed questions, adopt a style of facilitation that fits you, your desired outcome, and your organization. There are three spectrums along which you can consider facilitation style choices:

- Scripted or improvisational

- Spoken or visual

- Space-filling or space-making

Think of these styles as knobs that you can twist to adjust to the culture of an individual meeting. You naturally sit within each of these spectrums at a specific setting, but you may need to modify that setting to meet different challenges. You also might need to select a facilitator that has the strongest attributes in the desired style.

6

Better Meetings
Lead to Better
Organizations

Brian leads an engineering team in the U.S. government that helps federal agencies improve their digital services, including websites, apps, and any other services that citizens might access without getting or providing information on paper. Before joining this team, he managed a development team at a large Silicon Valley software company. One of the strongest aspects of the culture of that company was that solutions to problems were evaluated on their technical merits above all else. Software had to work very well and very fast. Part of his appeal to the federal agency was bringing that high performance philosophy to a similarly large, bureaucratic organization that historically had not been evaluated on performance.

103

The Office of Personnel keeps many data points about the various people employed by the federal government. Brian was part of a task force that was trying to normalize this information across multiple service points so that any time a service required a list of people or biographical information about those people, there was one place this information was updated and could be served to multiple places.

One of the project's challenges was the fact that different federal agencies categorized their employees using different terminology that often meant the same thing. While someone was classified as a "senior librarian" in one group, someone else serving an identical function might be tagged as a "lead archivist." This lack of normalization created real difficulties when employees wanted to generate lists across multiple groups. People would be excluded from a list when they shouldn't be, due to a lack of normalization.

Brian, representatives from his team, and a few subject matter experts met with the project sponsor at the Office of Personnel to explore the categorization. He found that no matter how he presented his case, the sponsor was resistant to reaching out to other federal organizations to ask them to change anything.

"I've been here a long time," the sponsor said, "and it's nearly impossible for us to change the way other people do things. If this is a priority, we'll have to do the heavy lifting on our end to create a separate list of categories and build relationships among all the variations."

Brian tuned out. He knew what was involved in the proposed approach because he'd seen it fail before. It also wouldn't be sustainable without the creation of new full-time positions to keep it up-to-date, but that funding didn't exist. Brian felt trapped between two cultures. He wanted to build sustainable solutions quickly within a slow, ancient, bureaucratic culture.

The Two Cultures

Every organization has two cultures. The first culture is the one that the organization aspires to have. You hear about that culture in advertising, job interviews, branding materials, and human resource orientations. The second is the culture that emerges and evolves over time, based on habits. This is the sometimes secret, but very real way in which things get done.

Over the past five chapters, you've learned about applying design to meetings to improve meeting outcomes. Better meeting outcomes, over time, improve organizations. The results you get, or don't get, from meetings are living evidence of those two cultures. By paying close attention to what goes on in meetings and using better design approaches to improve them, you can learn what a new job requires to be successful. You can create an environment that aligns with the culture you would like your employer to have, and even effect change in the culture, ultimately making you the best maker, manager, or anything you want to be. Meetings help you understand, build, and evolve your workplace. Effective organizations with good alignment between their aspirational and actual cultures have the capacity to change while continuing to achieve success without compromising their values.

Meetings Help You Understand a New Culture

People are job-hopping in the first five years after they graduate more than they ever did before.[1] When starting a new job, meetings are an invaluable way to understand how an organization works. In design research, usability testing tells you how well software works and where

---

1. Guy Berger, "Will This Year's College Grads Job-Hop More Than Previous Grads?" (Linkedin data analysis, 2016) https://blog.linkedin.com/2016/04/12/will-this-year_s-college-grads-job-hop-more-than-previous-grads

the pain points are. Meetings are usability tests for organizations themselves. Do they create an environment where it's easy to acclimate to necessary concepts and connect with solutions? Or do they obscure needed information in internal slang and ritual, purposeless gatherings?

Aaron Irizarry has learned to use meetings to acclimate to new organizations. Aaron has moved among a lot of large companies—organizations that range from thousands to hundreds of thousands of employees. Each time he's moved, the culture has been different. What worked well in meetings at each job depended on that company's unique structure and politics. Skills for participating in and running meetings didn't necessarily transfer from one job to the next seamlessly.

Aaron has found that design teams have a different level of political influence within each organization. Some teams work like a design agency within a company, seeking reviews and approvals. Others are more directly integrated into business and product strategic decisions. Communication styles vary based on the amount of political influence the design team wields.

"When I went into a new situation, I had a natural desire to prove myself." Aaron said. "I would think, 'Oh yeah, I know this.' I had to train myself to shut up and listen; see how the flow of meetings went; and see how people even did simple things, such as interoffice chat or email communications. I would watch how they communicated (in meetings)."

> *When you are new to your job, make an effort to observe more*
> *and speak less in your first several routine meetings.*
>
> **—AARON IRIZARRY**
> **HEAD OF EXPERIENCE INFRASTRUCTURE, CAPITAL ONE**

Early in a new position, Aaron adopted the position of being an observer. He paid attention to executives and product managers in discussions, to see when they responded positively. When contributing, he kept a list of previously observed successful behaviors in mind. As a manager, he also shared his findings from meetings with each new hire. As his employees went through the same transition he went through, he would step in and advocate, becoming a "meeting coach" when necessary. As the organization continued to evolve, he never stopped thinking of himself as a new employee, keeping his meeting observations going.

Meeting design will help you be more successful in a new job, but you can't design something without observing its constraints first. Observing, understanding, modeling, and eventually breaking an organization's behavior in meetings provides insights that will guide you to better outcomes. Meetings are also places where your value as a contributor can be seen, heard, and felt. Whether you are a new employee or a new consultant, meetings provide a window into what will work well and why. Ritual meetings and emergency get-togethers reveal embedded habits and assumptions of the organization. Navigating these habits and assumptions helps you get your point across when those meetings may need to change.

> *It's easier to adopt the language and vocabulary of the culture in which you are working than it is to teach them a new one.*
>
> **—DANA CHISNELL**
> **CODIRECTOR, CENTER FOR CIVIC DESIGN**

Our example, Brian, transitioned from one large, performance-driven culture to another large culture that was driven by a messy mix of criteria. In addition, Brian's job required him to regularly embed himself within a new agency and learn their way of doing things. In order to realize his goals more successfully, Brian should have observed how conversations drove the perception of a project. What did people talk about when something was working? How could he model his project's meetings around those behaviors?

How to Make a New Culture

New jobs don't always happen in pre-existing, large organizations. Sometimes, you find yourself in a fresh new organization, like a start-up company. Start-ups are new cultures, and new cultures are opportunities. From the beginning, you can have the kind of meetings you want and not waste time in ones that don't work well. Ironically, over time, those meetings will still become a habit and predictable, so that's why it's important to get them as close to right as you can when you start.

Meetings are an opportunity to provide a model of behavior that other people can replicate. Modeling gets more effective work out of a team than just telling people what to do. If you only act like a boss in the meetings you lead, then you set *your* agendas, push for *your* outcomes, and constrain the conversation to *your* views. This is leading with enforcement instead of modeling. Enforcing things in meetings prevents employees from learning by leading meetings themselves.

When Leslie Jensen-Inman and Jared Spool cofounded a new school for learning design, they recognized an opportunity to build the school's culture through meetings. They shared a passion for crafting the experience of learning. They expressed their shared values regularly and openly in early discussions, and those weekly explorations of values became part of normal operations. Those meetings also led Leslie to a powerful realization about their goals. "I needed to own (our culture). I started having one-on-one meetings with each of my direct reports every single week. I'm the one that's there all the time. I had to become a manager, which I wasn't before."

To be a great manager, Leslie investigated how to build the best culture for her team. She had to get as much right as possible on the first try, zeroing in on the best ways to handle the day-to-day business and the tone of being in the school. She identified positive and "value appropriate" behaviors, and then routinized those behaviors for herself and her employees in meetings. "A former professor taught me that once organizations set their values and culture at the very beginning, it's hard, if not impossible, to change that culture, unless you actually change the organization itself by changing all the leadership and hiring new people."

They identified what kinds of meeting experiences would represent their desired culture. Lifelong learning was an important value they wanted to instill. Although Leslie had become a manager, she spent little of her time in meetings actually managing. Instead she encouraged her employees in meetings by listening first and then pushing them beyond what they were comfortable expressing. Traditionally, a manager places boundaries on a discussion. Leslie instead pushed conversations further, like a coach.

Ultimately, Leslie distributed the responsibility of facilitation to a different staff member each meeting. "If someone wanted more practice running effective meetings, I gave that role to them. Running effective meetings is a marketable skill that's good for our employees while they are at our school, and great for them when they leave."

Staff meetings are a safe place to learn more about how to be an effective part of a team. By sharing and abdicating the role of facilitator, you enable lifelong learning. Meetings thrive when they are a safe, somewhat "unmanaged" place to practice facilitation and agenda design in the pursuit of outcomes. As Leslie said, "Our values and culture affect how we do our meetings. In effect, meetings are our culture—they bring it all together."

Changing a Culture

Brian from the federal government team was brought into his position to create a new culture, or probably more accurately, reinvigorate an old culture. But culture change is hard. Think about the culture of an established company with several years behind it. You're going to have people in leadership positions who carry the responsibility of the well-being of other people who depend on that organization to survive. Depending on how you feel about the role of government, it could be a whole population of citizens who depend on an organization to ensure their basic rights and maintain order, infrastructure, and the like.

When the bosses are in the meeting, it's a natural impulse to defer to them. If success is tied to someone having a favorable opinion of you, you are going to take their contributions to the conversation seriously. Over time, that deference can become ceremonial and cripple efficiency and innovation in meetings. But if you start from a position of connecting meetings to outcomes, and the leadership is aware of those outcomes, it creates an opportunity for culture change in meetings, through facilitation.

The opportunity created by facilitation is to confront leadership when their contribution is pulling you away from an agreed-upon meeting outcome. Although not all organizations have a mature facilitation practice, there are other ways that meetings can enable culture change when leadership seems stuck or off track. They can include establishing a regular exploratory conversation for questioning how things are done, working with an outside party (such as a consultant), and confronting a new or difficult challenge.

Exploring Change in Conversation

MailChimp is an email marketing and outreach software company that serves millions of organizations around the world. As MailChimp grew and became more successful, different divisions developed different approaches to evaluating their success. This resulted in valuable information becoming isolated in personal spreadsheets and documents that weren't readily accessible. Departments were unintentionally hoarding knowledge. In order to break down those barriers and increase transparency, the company instituted a weekly lunch meeting called the "data nerd lunch."

The data nerd lunch was open to anyone. Individuals from many departments presented datasets, described what created that data, and then reviewed what they had learned from analysis. After sharing, the group spent time providing feedback and guidance to the "data sharer" on how they might be able to take that analysis further.

The meeting increased the flow of information among MailChimp's departments. It even influenced new product features, when existing projects and initiatives took a slight shift in direction because of a small data insight or a bold question. When someone in the lunch meeting asked, "Wouldn't it be cool if we could see or do (a certain kind of analysis)," someone else would respond with "that's easy," or even the revelation that it was already done, but trapped in another department on someone's computer.

Typically, departments and subcultures silo knowledge to increase their influence and create an argument for increasing their budgets. However, at MailChimp, the opposite effect happened: departments that shared more became more influential. Sharing teams and departments were perceived as having critical insights. Aaron Walter described the change at MailChimp as "silos of information becoming increasingly porous. Teams that used data to help more people within the organization became more influential (than teams that didn't)."

Outsiders Opening the Door to Change

Organizations often don't see problems with meetings that are right in front of them. Some meetings become habitual ceremonies that serve little or no purpose. If the business doesn't take a turn for the worse, those habits will persist. However, an outside partner on a project can perceive problems to which in-house teams have become completely numb.

Aaron Parkening experienced this while working with an international architectural firm. As a project strategist, Aaron has a specific perspective on his role within meetings. He sees his job as making sure that everyone is comfortable, or uncomfortable if needed, to advance toward a meeting's outcome. He starts meetings with a clear statement of that intended meeting's outcome, and he immediately addresses any confusion about it before getting a conversation underway.

Aaron's client was a marketing department, and their work together was around the redesign and content governance for their websites. Before Aaron's work with the department, they characterized their meetings as lacking agendas, starting late, and never finishing on time. This process arose out of a tendency to tiptoe around the whims of executives, for the same self-preservation reasons discussed earlier in the chapter. When they started meetings, they were always ready to respond immediately to new ideas from the boss, whether they were valid or not. This led to habitually underplanned meetings, in order to save space for the executives' whims.

Aaron's approach to meetings was a revelation to his client. When a senior stakeholder challenged a meeting outcome statement at the start of a discussion, Aaron halted the meeting, captured the contrast between his views and the stakeholder's, and if necessary, said no. Saying no, or at least "not right now," was something the marketing team felt that they didn't have permission to do. When they saw that it could happen, it led to a sea change in the culture of their meetings that has stuck with them to this day.

Before Aaron's work with them, the group would spend unstructured meetings committing to things without considering them in a larger context. "Oh, that's something we can do in a week," they would promise in response to leadership identifying a "right now issue." But when they went back to work, they realized that they had overcommitted themselves in every single meeting. Now, they have a simple policy: they don't commit to any deadlines in meetings. Instead, they commit to tasks and then follow up later with deadlines when they can assess the tasks against a larger effort.

It's a small but powerful change in their culture. The marketing department is viewed as more effective than before because they are delivering more precisely on their promises. They've accrued more responsibility and grown their team and the quality of their work as a result. They credit this in part to "channeling the spirit of Aaron" in their ongoing meetings with leadership. And they still start with a statement of meeting outcomes and have an agenda for getting to those outcomes.

Sometimes, it just takes seeing what it could be like if you did things differently. A great place to see things differently is from the viewpoint of a person who doesn't have the history of habits that your organization has accrued.

Finding Change by Confronting Problems

Aaron's architectural firm client didn't challenge doing business as usual because their business was healthy. But what if business took a turn for the worse, or an organization was confronted with a serious challenge? A meeting where you confront a problem in all its ugly glory can help an organization change its culture.

Jesse Taggert successfully helped a federal government agency confront one of those ugly problems. In the process, her team made significant changes in the way that agency could get its work done, saving time and money and improving the experience of their customers. She did this by convening a workshop with the right group of people and visualizing a problem together.

Design consultants like Jesse often do visualization in workshops using sketches and sticky notes. But outside of design organizations or design projects, this way of working is seen as revolutionary. One reason this exists in government agencies is that the culture is driven by a strong fear of accountability; as a result, they are more averse to risk. Processes lock themselves down into "just effective enough" workflows without ever questioning the way that things are done. Over time, individuals who facilitate that workflow become isolated from the overall process into silos.

One agency that Jesse worked with was responsible for providing certifications that allowed businesses to hire and support people with severe disabilities. Workflow rigidity around the certification process led to responsible subgroups being disconnected from an awareness of the overall flow. This slowed the process down, resulting in a backlog of more than 700 applications.

Jesse designed a three-day workshop with the intent of pulling all those subsets of people together to map the whole certification flow, prototype revisions to the process, and discuss those prototypes. Civil servants, who had never met before in person but whose work was deeply intertwined, gathered together in a single room. Over the course of the workshop, solutions were created that helped these groups find new energy. When agency leadership came in at the end to review what had been developed, it was as though their employees had been replaced with a new, more motivated team.

Changes in the service were made that improved efficiency in processing applications, created digital self-service tools, and eliminated simple redundancies. Within six weeks of the workshop, putting those new ideas and processes into place lowered the standing backlog of applications from 700 to fewer than 150, and they have maintained that improvement. More importantly, they realized that taking risks through exploratory, collaborative effort could help them do their jobs better.

Well-designed meetings obviously won't fix a culture every time. Sometimes, it requires an alignment of problems and a smart person to facilitate the exploration of them. But Jesse and her team used a meeting to help people examine embedded assumptions that could be very hard to extract. Changing an organization is tough because it can require upending habits that are perceived as required.

As one of the leading thinkers in new approaches to content and design, Karen McGrane knows this firsthand. She has coached dozens of organizations on how to manage change within their web teams to respond to a continually evolving landscape of devices and techniques.

HOW CAN I ORIENT PEOPLE TO NEW WAYS OF DOING THINGS IN A CONVERSATION?

Karen McGrane
Managing Partner, Bond Art + Science and author of
Content Strategy for Mobile** and **Going Responsive

Karen plays nicely in the content strategy, information architecture, and interaction design sandboxes. She is a managing partner at Bond Art + Science, a UX consultancy she founded in 2006, and formerly VP and National Lead for User Experience at Razorfish. She also teaches design management in the Interaction Design MFA program at the School of Visual Arts. Her two books, Going Responsive *and* Content Strategy for Mobile, *were published by A Book Apart.*

The web is nothing but change. Every year, it seems like there's a new tool, a new process, a new shiny-whizbang-must-have. I can see why web design teams start to resist (or even fear) changing something that's working for them.

Enter an explosion of mobile devices. Teams can't design and manage websites the old way because people don't look at the web the old way. New screen sizes, form factors, and capabilities on smartphones and tablet devices represent one of the biggest transformations that web teams have ever been through. Users have adopted these new devices wholeheartedly, and it's clear that the teams that own the websites must keep up.

And yet . . . they don't. It's been ten years since the initial launch of the iPhone, and many organizations still don't have a mobile website that meets customer needs. It has been seven years since Ethan Marcotte first wrote about responsive web design, and yet most organizations' sites haven't gone responsive. The barrier to change isn't touchscreens or even fluid grids and media queries—it's orienting the entire team to change the way they work.

CONTINUES ➤

CONTINUED ➤

When Orienting People to Change

I've consulted with dozens of companies along the road to responsive design, and change management is a big part of the job. Along the way, I've learned the following:

- Don't make people feel dumb.

  Mobile has changed the landscape and introduced new tools and terminology. Even experienced web professionals can feel out of their league sometimes. Spend time setting levels and building a shared understanding—don't assume everyone has the same baseline of knowledge.

- Data isn't a magic wand.

  If data were all it took to persuade people to change, I could put up a few charts showing eye-popping increases in mobile traffic and then take an early lunch. Data can bolster an argument or direct the team's focus, but it won't persuade someone who isn't ready to change. Some teams cling to data as if it will magically change people's minds, but it won't.

- You can't argue your way through fear.

  Making big changes to the website is risky, and people's professional reputations (and even jobs) are on the line. No one will admit this in a meeting, so they wrap themselves in arguments and logic that serves them (even if it isn't the right direction). You'll never win that debate with logic if you don't also address their unspoken fears.

- Motivate by fixing pain points.

  The most effective change happens when teams identify something that's caused them problems—maybe even something they were so accustomed to doing that they didn't even realize how painful it was. Articulating that pain and offering a solution is powerfully motivating.

Change in Practice: Responsive Design

For example, I see many teams struggle with reviewing work-in-progress with stakeholders. People expect to review fully rendered web pages mocked up in Photoshop before they'll approve the design or content. Working this way is inefficient and error-prone, but teams are so accustomed to working this way that they almost don't see it as a problem.

In a responsive design process, teams simply can't work that way anymore. But design and development teams that want to move to creating prototypes also need buy-in from the rest of the organization. By tapping into the pain and problems associated with time-consuming reviews of static comps, teams are more likely to want to move to a new way of working.

It's obvious that mobile has changed the landscape of the web. What's less obvious is the way it changes the way teams work. Organizations move slowly, but change can happen. Show empathy for the struggles of your stakeholders and your team, and then frame the change you propose within those very struggles.

Amplify the Best of a Culture

A well-designed conversation will help departments make decisions about what their process or organization might need to change. But those decisions can still turn out to be wrong. An ending meeting, like a postmortem, can address process breakdowns without becoming awkward or painful, if done correctly.

Etsy customizes its postmortems to prevent the blame game in final reviews. They believe that circumstances, not people, are to blame for failures. This belief is part of what they call a "just culture." When things go wrong, rather than immediately reprimanding the accountable party, they try to understand the thought process that led to a mistake. They assume people will always do what they think is right based on the knowledge that they have at the time. Etsy positions failure as part of the learning process.

Etsy's Chief Information Officer John Allspaw says a just culture "balances safety with accountability."[2] The result is that the people who are closest to the problem feel comfortable being transparent about what happened. As a result, Etsy gets a better understanding of the complex causes of system failures. They call their postmortem meetings "blameless" and follow a deliberate recipe for conversation around things going wrong.

Having a blameless postmortem includes five steps.

1. All parties involved give a detailed account of what actions they took at what time.

2. They share what effects they observed.

3. They discuss what expectations they had.

4. They review assumptions they had made.

5. They go over their understanding of the timeline of events as they occurred.

---

2. John Allspaw, "Blameless Postmortems and a Just Culture," Etsy, Code as Craft (blog), May 22, 2012, https://codeascraft.com/2012/05/22/blameless-postmortems/

The participants give this detailed account without fear of "punishment or retribution."[3] This method rewards getting the details of the story correct over identifying a culprit. Learning from failure is a complex interaction between our ability to understand that failure and our tendency to reduce the way we look at a system correction as just a process of removing bad actors. Sydney Dekker calls this the "bad apple" theory, which states that an organization should improve if you simply remove those so-called bad apples.[4]

The poor choices that people make aren't usually due to being bad apples. People arrive at an unanticipated failure or take a risk that doesn't pay off, but in the story of the failure is the information that could have prevented it. Examining why failure takes place without the fear of losing one's job leads to insights that enable an organization to overcome that failure in the future.

Etsy's policy highlights the fact that they value improvements in the process over the short-term elimination of people who make mistakes. It's about making a team more sustainable and self-educating. That's exactly the kind of team you want to be on, and it's exactly the kind of person you want to be: always open to becoming better.

Anger in Meetings

Unfortunately, there are meetings where someone loses their cool. Expressions of anger in meetings can damage an organization long after that meeting is over. Relationships fracture and eventually break, and that will start to manifest in the work. But why does it happen? When human beings feel threatened, they use whatever tools they have to do what they believe is best for the success, or the survival, of their group. One of those tools is anger. When the anger is directed at you,

---

3. Ibid.
4. Sidney Dekker, *The Field Guide to Understanding Human Error*, rev. ed. (Burlington, VT: Ashgate, 2006).

it helps if you can remember that anger is coming from good intentions. It will help you keep your cool even when others cannot.

A person can be at their worst even while they believe they are doing the right thing. You may see their "right thing" as inappropriate, selfish, or destructive. As hard as it may be, try to meet people where the problem lies by taking the time to understand what leads them to their conclusions rather than debating those conclusions. Adopting this mindset helps you forgive yourself and others, for the very human, emotional reactions you have when things get tense.

Applying what you've learned in Part 1, "The Theory and Practice of Meeting Design," will help you overcome the problems of habitual, unproductive, and ill-considered meetings. When difficult meetings happen, meeting design helps you keep your head clear, your arguments logical, and your approach flexible. It works because meetings and the culture they exist within are inseparable. That's why meetings are a powerful tool to build, understand, celebrate, and when necessary, change your culture.

WHAT YOU NEED TO KNOW

The meetings in an organization describe, define, and have the capability to change that organization's culture. Being aware of the relationship between meetings and culture helps you use meetings as a tool to assess a variety of things, and make change.

- Meetings help new employees understand the difference between what an organization *believes* its culture is like and how things really get done.

- Managers can be explicit about the kinds of behavior they want to encourage in meetings, as a way of creating a culture that reflects the organization's values. You can demonstrate trust by letting anyone facilitate a meeting, regardless of their status in the organization. For meetings that analyze failure, identify assumptions and reward strategic thinking even if it's wrong, as opposed to threatening blame and repercussions.

- Experiment with regular meetings around shared goals or practices involving attendees across departments that don't normally work together. It removes knowledge barriers that exist between groups that arise out of the segmentation of workflow among departments.

- Sometimes it takes an outside perspective to change inside practices in your meetings. It's hard to recognize an opportunity to improve when you live in the same meeting each and every day.

2

Designed Meetings

Here are several starter agendas for common types of meetings. They are categorized by where they fall in the lifecycle of your work: near the beginning, in the middle, or at the end of a project or process. Your work life makes it difficult to build purposeful agendas every single time you get together, for obvious reasons. I've built them on a foundation of measurable outcomes and baked in meeting design constraints from the theory and practice of meeting design.

Think of the remainder of this book as a basic cookbook, rather than a recipe book. It's a selection of different flavors and components of a larger agenda from which you can pull as you see fit. Find an agenda that loosely fits what you need and then customize it in the context of your goals and your team. Save time by first starting with the facilitation directions provided, if that's enough to get results. When you really need to adapt an approach, focus on your facilitation strategy and style within these approaches.

In each chapter, meetings are presented roughly in the order in which they might take place. But different contexts will merit revisiting that sequence, skipping certain meetings, or changing things more drastically.

7

Get Started with Beginning Meetings

G reat kickoff experiences and other beginning meetings can happen with intentional design. Sadly, however, these meetings are frequently used only to bookend a project plan. In design agencies, getting that kickoff meeting on the calendar helps ensure a project deposit payment. But those same agencies often put very little thought into those early meetings. Surely, we can just get everyone in a room and figure out what to address, right? It's hard enough to get these things on the calendar.

Although it is challenging to book that first meeting, a bad first meeting means even more of a difficult course correction down the line. When time spent together at the beginning of a project is well-considered, fewer revisions (and hours) are required later, saving time and money for everyone involved. In addition, establishing trust and camaraderie at the beginning of a relationship is the fuel that moves a relationship through the unpredictable challenges.

> *Always start off a meeting by very explicitly stating the meeting's purpose. This helps people who don't understand why they're there. Then always end by asking if there was anything they felt we should cover that we didn't. It creates a safe space to uncover missed opportunities and hidden assumptions.*
>
> —KAREN MCGRANE
> MANAGING PARTNER, BOND ART + SCIENCE AND
> AUTHOR, *CONTENT STRATEGY FOR MOBILE AND GOING RESPONSIVE*

The Sales Meeting

The sales process for a product or service creates a tone that contributes to or prevents success. Good sales conversations lead to happy working relationships, while awkward ones cost you the possibility of working with someone now and far into the future. If you've gotten to the point of getting a sales meeting on the calendar, there's no question that the capability to do the job is there—the sales meeting is about assessing for a fit.

Goal of a Sales Meeting

Sales meetings are like dating. The goal for both parties is to assess the fit of a relationship on an effort. When the fit is right, you'll want to invest more in the relationship, find more opportunities to work together, and celebrate what aspects of the fit are making things go well. If the fit is not ideal, you'll want to leave the door open for other possible opportunities by avoiding burning bridges (unless it's a terrible, horrible fit). During a sales meeting, that relationship can go from being an acquaintance to becoming a candidate, or from being a candidate to winning a competitive sales bid. Sales meetings can also be used to connect one successful effort to the next potential project.

Sales meetings fail when they aren't designed to assess fit. Like a date, if you try too hard and jump into more intimate details prematurely, such as project schedule or budget, it doesn't work. There's not good alignment of ideas between parties, because you aren't talking about things at the same level of complexity.

Sales meetings that go well leave everyone wanting to continue the conversation. You book the next meeting and are eager to get started. Both parties conceptualize an actionable, shared idea, and roughly agree on the value of that idea.

Measuring the Outcome of a Sales Meeting

The outcome you should seek from a sales meeting is a deeper relationship. This can only be measured by assessing where the relationship is before the meeting. A successful measure could be as simple as the presence of a returned phone call or email, or it could be as complex as someone requesting a statement of work, providing a deposit check, and setting up a services agreement. Go into a sales meeting with a few ideas about what an appropriate indicator of the next logical step in the relationship could be.

SAMPLE AGENDA FOR A SALES MEETING (60 MINUTES)

Sales meetings vary wildly with what services or products are being sold and at what scale, so you'll need to adapt this to the kind of work you do. But at the core, it's always a meeting to assess the fit between two parties, and this structure addresses that goal. This agenda assumes that the vendor has done some preliminary work to define the problem beforehand, and they are looking to seal the deal.

Introductions (10 minutes)

Each attendee provides their name, their role in their respective organization, and one question they have about this effort. Capture this visually on a whiteboard or large easel.

CONTINUES ➤

CONTINUED ➤

Positioning Statement (15 minutes)

The vendor provides a brief rationale for the proposed process, product, or solution. It should consist of no more than five key points about the product or solution without excessive detail. Those points should focus on differentiators compared to other options the prospective client might have. The vendor should state their position simply, but be prepared to provide details when asked.

Positioning Reflection (15 minutes)

The vendor reviews each key point and asks for feedback along the way. It's important to use good question design to facilitate discussion, such as the following:

- "This proposal is based on assumptions we've made about your business. Are those assumptions correct?"
- "What does the best possible outcome look like on this project?"
- "Describe what happens after the engagement is over. How will this work help you overcome a specific problem, grow, and thrive?"

Related Project or Portfolio Review (10 minutes)

The vendor should review previous work with other clients, or how their proposed solution has worked well for other companies. For each example, the vendor should provide a statement on how each item relates to the client's work, now as well as in the future.

Related Project Questions and Final Review of Initial Questions (10 minutes)

Touch upon a small selection of questions from the beginning of the meeting. For the in-person conversation, it should be no more than five or six. Remaining questions can be pulled from unanswered questions out of the initial collection and be the subject of a follow-up email. Identify any other follow-up actions for both the client and the vendor before leaving the room.

HOW CAN I BALANCE BEING GENUINE AND BEING SUCCESSFUL IN A SALES MEETING?

Giles Colborne
Managing Director, cxpartners

Giles is the author of Simple and Usable, Web, Mobile, and Interaction Design *and founder and managing director of cxpartners, a digital consultancy that excels in user-centered design and collaborative methods.*

The problem with sales conversations is that people think the purpose is to persuade, or worse, manipulate someone into buying something. That's a terrible approach. If you're trying to make someone do something against their best interests, then you'll leave a trail of disappointment and resentment behind you. Over time, your reputation and your peace of mind will suffer.

Good sales conversations are about helping people with their problems. But even with the right mindset, there are three things that people forget to do.

1. **Just listen.**

   The first is to begin by listening. Most people think they need to start by showing off their credentials, making themselves sound important and justifying their seat at the table. I cringe when I watch old videos of myself starting presentations like this. No matter how well intended, it's like going to a party and being cornered by someone boasting about their kids, or their car, or their holiday.

   Your best justification for being part of the conversation is that you care about the person you're talking to. The best way to show that is to listen, ask questions, and be genuinely interested in the other person.

   Start by telling the other person why you're interested in their situation. ("I'm always interested to hear how people go about designing a new app because I always learn something new.") Keep asking for more details and keep listening. The more you learn, the better you'll be able to help later on.

CONTINUES ➤

CONTINUED ➤

As you're listening, you'll probably start to hear what you think are problems; don't assume that means your client wants to buy from you.

A couple of years ago, I met a potential client who told me he thought the new designs for his ecommerce website would do a worse job at sales conversion than his existing ones. To me, that sounded like a big problem. But he was unconcerned. He was sure that "growth in the market" would make up for the dip in sales conversion. Besides, he liked the look of the new designs. It was clear he really wasn't interested in hearing how I could make his website more effective, and the conversation could go no further. This was the best possible outcome for both of us.

2. **Confirm investment in the problem.**

The second thing you should do in a sales conversation is to make sure that your client agrees that the problem is worth solving. Even experienced salespeople forget to do this: they rush in with a solution that the client may not value at all, and the rest of the conversation is a desperate attempt to convince the client to buy.

Instead, when you think you've identified a pain point, you must poke it to see if it really hurts. Ask "What are the consequences of that?" It seems cruel, but keep on poking. Ask "Does that have a

Stakeholder Interviews

Project stakeholders are people in senior leadership positions who can "thumbs up" or "thumbs down" an idea. Conducting interviews with stakeholders to inform agendas will set expectations and identify gaps in thinking before critical meetings. They should usually be the first negative effect for your team?" or "Would that matter in your performance review?" or "Does that stop you from solving your other problems?" and so on. What you're interested in is finding reasons why this might be an important problem and if the solution is worth the time, money, and effort required.

3. **Ask if you can help.**

Only then can you can move on to the third task: asking permission to help. It's just good manners. Demonstrate that you listened carefully (by playing back some relevant details), determine if the problem is worth solving (by recalling the pain points), and ask if you can offer a solution. As long as you explain your solution simply and clearly, there's no "selling" required.

Of course, the *best* solution may not be *your* solution. Sometimes, someone doesn't need a new car; they just need a taxi home. Try to be honest with yourself about whether you're best placed to fix their problem. If you aren't the best choice, you'll gain trust and build a stronger relationship if you find someone else to help rather than mis-selling your services.

To build that relationship, take the pressure off the conversation. Make sure that this isn't the only sales opportunity you have before you walk in the door. If you know you have three or four other conversations lined up, you make it easier to stop treating people as "sales opportunities" and start treating them as human beings.

meeting in a project. A kickoff meeting without getting to know an organization's goals and culture, as seen by those making decisions, risks being a waste of time. Understanding stakeholder perspectives will help everyone home in on what can and must be done.

Goal of Stakeholder Interviews

The goal of any stakeholder interview is to assess alignment between your understanding and a stakeholders' understanding of the work. This can require establishing a high degree of transparency with someone you may have just met, so it needs to go beyond following a script of questions and recording answers. Find a light personal connection with the subject to establish a friendly "off-the-record" tone. That tone leads the conversation to more honest assumptions about outcomes and risks. Most of the interview should consist of a small set of clear and direct questions, with room to explore among them. Be sure to ask what aspects of organizational culture, what internal processes, or which team members could put success at risk.

Measuring the Outcome of Stakeholder Interviews

Individual interviews with stakeholders as a preparatory method for larger meetings can be a tough sell because they feel like "meetings before the meeting." They can also be tough to schedule with busy people. But conversations with stakeholders are a sifting process. In an hour-long conversation, you will get different amounts of value. You might only collect three or four thoughts in an interview that refine your project goals. But by compiling those thoughts across multiple stakeholders and comparing them to your initial plan, you'll learn a lot of necessary information. It tells you where leadership has gaps in understanding among the various parties and against your team's vision. A good measure of success for these meetings is the number of gaps you identify. The more gaps that help you refine your plans, the better.

It's important to remember, however, that as you identify a gap in an interview, that is not the best time to address that gap. Differences in expectations are what you collect to build a great project kickoff workshop. Don't spend interviews trying to allay stakeholders' fears; don't argue with people when you are there to listen.

SAMPLE AGENDA FOR STAKEHOLDER INTERVIEW (30 MINUTES TO 60 MINUTES)

Introduction (5 minutes max)

Establish the purpose of the conversation. Assure the interviewee that your goal is to listen, not talk. If you intend to record the subject, get permission on the call or in writing, depending on the laws where you happen to be conducting the interview. (Laws vary on the requirements of permission to be recorded, so be clear on the laws that apply to you.)

Suggested Questions (25 to 55 minutes)

Be sure these questions suit the specific requirements of your project.

- Tell me about your role at [organization name].
- Tell me about your vision for the work you do at [organization name].
- What is the most important way that this project will change this organization?
- From your perspective, what are some of the critical audiences for [this project]?
- If you had to choose one, who would you say is the primary audience?
- What are the most important types of information that [this project] requires in order to be successful?
- What kinds of information do you need that you don't have yet?
- What are the most important things people can do or actions they can take because of [this project]?
- Are there annual or business cycles of activity that could change how the audiences behave? If so, please describe those cycles. What kind of information falls outside of those cycles?
- What role does [this project] play in the [organization name]'s business strategy?
- What puts [this project] at risk to fail?
- What is the one thing you must get right to make the project worth undertaking?
- Assuming that we mitigate any risks you've identified, what would make [this project] a wildly successful project?

The "Quickoff:" A Quick Kickoff Meeting

Good collaboration at the beginning of a project will almost always result in savings down the line. For that reason, rushed, short kick-off meetings can be a waste of time. Everyone comes to the table with preconceived notions based on limited knowledge about goals, and the resulting tendency is to blend everyone's baggage into goals for the project. But people are busy and still need to get projects started with a limited amount of time to get on the same page. Here's a meeting to use when you find yourself in that situation.

Goal of a Quickoff

The goal of a quick kickoff meeting is to confirm shared assumptions and identify project risks. Anything beyond this, such as exploring possible concepts or approaches, requires more than an hour. If you start this meeting and find that you can't get through confirming shared assumptions (e.g., you have different expectations of project outcomes), congratulations! You have identified your first project risk. The fact that people may not be on the same page about a project is just evidence that a more involved discussion is required, but don't worry—you've still met the goal of the meeting, even if that's the only risk you've identified.

A successful, brief kickoff meeting requires a pretty hefty amount of preparation. A full project brief describing outcomes and detailed phases or sprint plans should be provided at least two days prior to the meeting, because there's no room for any exploratory tangents or unmanaged, unproductive conflict in a short meeting like this.

Measuring the Outcome of a Quickoff

If the meeting ends with some clear action items and associated deadlines, then it has served its purpose. The meeting's quality can be measured by the quantity of action items generated and the distribution of those items to attending parties. If the quantity of action items is low, then the meeting didn't do a good job of aligning assumptions and risks with actions that people can take. If the action items are distributed equitably but someone leaves the meeting without anything to do, then there were some people in attendance who didn't need to be there.

SAMPLE AGENDA FOR A QUICKOFF (60 MINUTES)

A brief project kickoff establishes by phase (or by sprint) what is expected of all project parties. This example agenda assumes three sprints or phases. If you aren't involved in one or more of these sprints or phases, there's no reason for you to attend a meeting like this. This meeting is about building team cohesion and clarity quickly; there's no time for wandering. It also assumes that the overall purpose of the project has already been determined.

Project Process Overview (10 minutes)

Identify the beginning and end of each major project step; however, these steps are divided. If they are done in phases based on delivery of documentation (e.g., deliverables), identify when the final document will arrive, and when it will be approved and by whom. If it is an agile process, identify the goal of each sprint and who is accountable to declare if a goal has been achieved.

Process Phase/Sprint Focus (7–8 minutes)

Review the first sprint or phase in the project sequence in detail, identifying key decisions and associated decision-makers. If the phase includes multiple iterations on a document or design, discuss each iteration's goals, and who can declare that the goal has been achieved.

CONTINUES ➤

CONTINUED ➤

As each person is assigned action items in the phase/sprint, have them write down each action item and their initials on a different color of sticky note, and post those notes in sequence on a writable surface such as paper taped to a wall or a whiteboard (see Figure 7.1). If there are enough colors for everyone in the group, it helps to use a different color for each person.

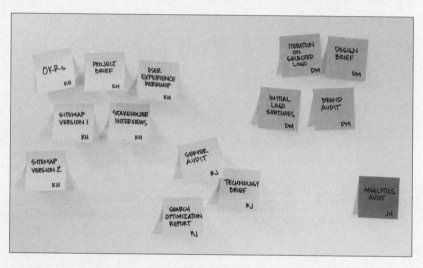

FIGURE 7.1 Collaborate to represent your project visually in a brief kickoff meeting called a *quickoff*.

Process Phase/Sprint Review (7–8 minutes)

Review the shared sticky notes and add a new color of notes to capture additional questions and dependencies. For each action item you've identified, ask the following two questions. First, how will this be achieved? Discuss and capture any additional steps that emerge. Second, does this depend on something else being achieved first? If it does, draw a line between the two items that have a dependent relationship (see Figure 7.2).

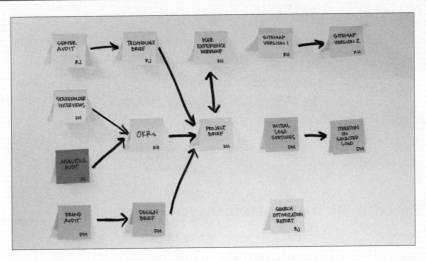

FIGURE 7.2 It helps to have a surface on which you can draw to identify dependencies.

Repeat the Focus and Review steps for each phase/sprint of the project. In this example, there are two additional phases, so that would total around 30 additional minutes.

Document the final process map by taking a photo (panoramic, if necessary) and have everyone take their own personal notes off the wall (or just photograph them) as a record of their action items. Make any updates to the central documentation of the project plan (e.g., personal kanban board/cards, or to-do lists in the project management software flavor of your choice). The example seen in Figure 7.3 uses Trello.

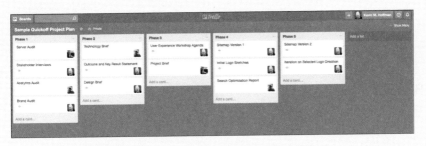

FIGURE 7.3 A quickoff meeting's result captured in a process management tool, in this case Trello.

Brainstorming

The value of brainstorming is debated, and the practice of brainstorming is defined in different ways and approached with different levels of rigor. There are convincing arguments for it being ineffective at generating new or good ideas.[1] Yet brainstorming endures as a catchy term used to describe the purpose of a meeting. In this case, brainstorming is defined as a collaborative process to generate a high volume of ideas, which increases the odds of having a successful idea.

The Goal of Brainstorming

The goal of a brainstorming meeting is like the goal of a good camping experience. Campers have a simple rule about a campsite: leave it in better shape than you found it. Brainstorming meetings where the group is no better off than they were before are unacceptable. But the opposite—the hope that you are leaving the room with the one, perfect idea—is not a good goal either. The goal is to leave with more viable solutions than you had before, but without becoming fixated on one of them. No one spends an entire camping trip cleaning and landscaping to create the perfect campsite for the next group to use it.

Measuring the Outcome of Brainstorming

There are two ways to measure the outcome of brainstorming. The first, most critical and most obvious measurement is the quantity of ideas collected. But it's not a race to get to the biggest number. Leaving the room without some effort toward assessing the quality of those ideas would be a mistake. The second, therefore, is attaching a simple, easily applied measure of viability to each idea. The best brainstorming meetings increase the quantity of *viable* options.

---

1. Rebecca Greenfield, "Brainstorming Doesn't Work; Try This Technique Instead," *Fast Company,* July 29, 2014, https://www.fastcompany.com/3033567/agendas/brainstorming-doesnt-work-try-this-technique-instead

An option is viable if you have solid agreement about the problem that you are trying to solve. A good brainstorming session should spend as much time building agreement on what the problem is as adding detail to that problem. A meeting only filled with a discussion of solutions is likely to leave a few attendees feeling like the viability of some of those solutions is suspect. Here's an agenda that creates that balance of quantity and quality.

> *If you are doing a group voting exercise, such as dot voting,*
> *eliminate speaking to reduce uneven power dynamics.*
>
> —DANA CHISNELL
> CODIRECTOR, CENTER FOR CIVIC DESIGN

SAMPLE BRAINSTORMING AGENDA (10 MINUTES TO 60 MINUTES)

This sample agenda is based on the KJ method, a technique for exploring group priorities developed by Jiro Kawakita in the 1960s.[2] In this example, sticky notes and markers enable the group to capture their own group memory without the designation of a meeting recorder.

This agenda scales well to the complexity of the topic being brainstormed. Simple brainstorms can be done in as few as 10 minutes, while multifaceted brainstorms can and should take much longer. This agenda also works well for larger groups when additional facilitation support is present. A single facilitator for every six attendees or so is sufficient.

Introduction (Up to 15 minutes)

Present the group with a single focusing question or statement that you will be exploring for the session. That question should be discussed for specificity and any areas of confusion among participants so that each party has the same idea of what constraints are implied by the question. Be sure to remove or revise any leading questions. Instead of phrasing a question like "Why can't this solution work for this problem?" think more like "What *could* work for solving this problem?"

CONTINUES ➤

---

2. Kai Yang, *Voice of the Customer Capture and Analysis* (New York: McGraw-Hill Education, 2008).

CONTINUED ➤

Generation (5–10 minutes)

Spend five minutes freely listing ideas, with one idea written largely and clearly as a simple statement on a single Post-it Note. Encourage people not to provide too much detail. Instead, provide an example of the appropriate amount of detail to help them think about how much to write.

Then spend five minutes posting all notes in a shared space on the wall. Post the answers for each single question in close proximity to one another. Don't worry about it being pretty, because you're going to move these things around (see Figure 7.4).

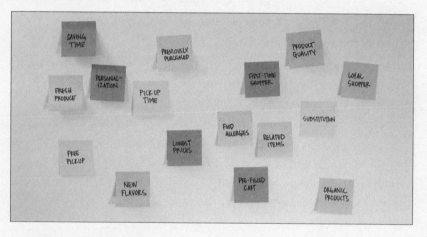

FIGURE 7.4 KJ brainstorming prior to evaluation.

Evaluation (10 minutes)

Spend five minutes grouping similar or identical notes in the same physical space on the wall so that if someone is browsing they wouldn't find similar notes too far apart from each other. If you like, you can provide labels for the groups. This is helpful if you've got several groups (let's say more than five), or if there are groups that have sufficient ambiguity to consider collapsing them or breaking them apart. Once everything is grouped (and labeled, if you choose), begin exercising judgment by using "dot voting" or another similar technique.

What Is Dot Voting?

Dot voting is a technique that allows a group to express priorities without talking. Decide on the number of "votes" that people can have: three to five votes is a good place to start, depending on the number of ideas across which votes are distributed. For each idea, have people add dots to the ones they find the most promising by applying a "dot" with a marker or using architectural tape dots (see Figure 7.5). They can distribute their dots across multiple solutions or use as many of their dots in one place as they like. The goal is to express a group evaluation of possible solutions visually, without talking it to death.

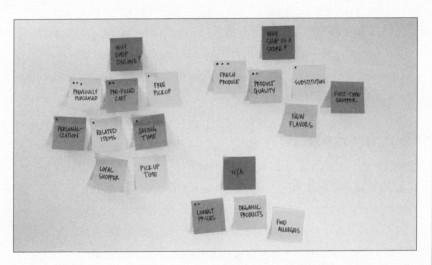

FIGURE 7.5 KJ brainstorming after some evaluation, including dot voting.

Discussion and Closure (10 to 15 minutes, optional)

If you'd like to move further in the process, review what options were the most popular with the group. Now is the time to discuss any results of dot voting—including pros and cons—by going around the table. Open, unstructured discussion is another good way to decompress. Focus on eliminating any weak options as opposed to arguing the relative merits of a single solution. That way, you'll have that successful camping trip and leave the room with more viable ideas than when you started.

Strategy Discussions Using Objectives and Key Results Statements (OKRs)

Sometimes a team is so focused on what they are making that they don't (or can't) discuss why they are making it. An isolated discussion on strategy near the beginning of a project focuses on the why without the what, and builds ways for measuring the effectiveness of the what. But talking about strategy poses a challenge. Many people discuss strategy in terms of finished products and end states. One of the hardest things about discussing a strategy is to distinguish it from related tactics. Bread-baking experts might consider using warmer water in the dough. This is a tactic, and it's easier to conceptualize and discuss than the scientific reason why that might prevent the bread from collapsing in the middle of baking.

What Is an OKR?

A strategy discussion should tie behavior to purpose. Both behavior (the thing you do) and purpose (why you do it) are important, but it's difficult to clearly link behavior to purpose in discussion or writing. Objectives and Key Results statements[3] (OKRs) accomplish the link. Companies such as Intel and Google develop OKRs to create a measurable connection between the measurable results of a specific effort and larger organizational goals. OKRs help teams focus and prioritize around a specific outcome: the objective. An objective statement is qualitative. It should be ambitious but vague, and occasionally uncomfortable because it forces you to reflect on your own assumptions. An objective is paired with quantitatively measured key results, sometimes in groups of three.[4] Good key results are hard to reach but not unrealistic.

---

3. Andrew Grove, *High Output Management* (New York: Vintage, 1995).
4. Christina Wodtke, *Radical Focus: Achieving Your Most Important Goals with Objectives and Key Results* (Boxes & Arrows, 2016).

Goal of an OKR Meeting

A great strategic meeting starts by building agreement about objectives. Any immediate discussion of key results should be minimized or labeled as a distraction. No matter how important people believe those key results are, they should be captured in a parking lot, as seen in Figure 7.6, for later discussion.

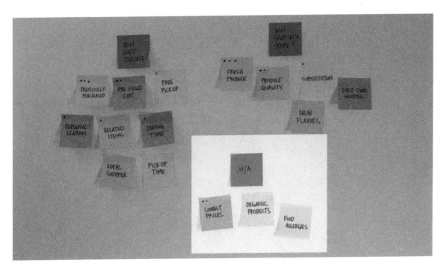

FIGURE 7.6 The parking lot, highlighted on the lower right, is a place to capture important ideas that aren't relevant to the immediate discussion.

Measuring the Outcome of an OKR Meeting

When using OKRs to structure discussions about strategy, the meeting's outcome is measured as the amount of clarity about the objective(s). Discussions that consist of ambitious, vague ideas are fertile ground for many tangents. While those tangents are necessary, at some point, you'll have to facilitate convergence toward that clarity. A successful discussion of objectives will zero in on ones that have the most potential: the ones that align well with the organization's mission but still feel within the realm of possibility.

SAMPLE AGENDA FOR AN OKR MEETING (2 HOURS)

Frame the Problem (20 minutes)

This meeting's job is to build good strategy. A good strategy puts resources (people, money, and time) to use in the most effective fashion toward an improved solution to a problem. Having this meeting at all implies that there's a problem with the current way of using resources. In advance of the OKR meeting, the facilitator should provide a full background on the problem, which describes the following:

- **Current Key Results:** The current measures of the existing outcome and why those results are unacceptable.

- **Resources:** All the resources that are used in support of the strategy.

- **Principal Constraints:** List only permanent aspects of the situation; the ones that cannot be changed (don't include *all* constraints, just significant ones).

- **Existing Strategy:** The way in which those resources and constraints are currently being utilized and managed, respectively.

Don't mention potential new strategies in the documentation, because the point of the meeting is to build new strategies collaboratively. Spend five minutes reviewing the document and then allow each person to ask up to three questions about the existing strategy. Record questions where everyone can see them for the duration of the discussion and reflect (repeat aloud) any answers to the group. Rely on the group to answer those questions. If you are the facilitator, you shouldn't be the only one speaking, if you speak that much at all.

Capture All Constraints (30 minutes)

Spend 10 minutes helping people capture additional constraints—anything that affects the problem. Everyone can write one constraint per sticky note with a big legible marker using simple descriptive phrases or statements. The goal of this part of the activity is to capture all constraints that may exist outside of the permanent, salient ones you've already identified prior to the meeting. At first, this may be slow—it may require an example or two to get people started.

Get no more than five new constraints from each person and then have them post those constraints to the wall. As they post them, have them provide a verbal explanation of each one to the group. Having people post one person at a time will prevent duplicate constraints from being added. Let people know that duplicates aren't necessary, but if someone has a variant, ask that person to rewrite it so that it's described differently.

Once all constraints are posted, you can optionally spend another 10 minutes grouping similar constraints together and giving each group a label. Write the labels of all constraint groups in a big list that's easily viewable.

Remove Constraints (30 minutes)

For each constraint group, capture the effect it has on the problem, using the labels of minimal, notable, or significant. *Significant* constraints have the largest effect on the problem, *notable* have modest effects, and *minimal* have the smallest effect. To collect this assessment from the room, use architectural dots (stickers) in three colors (see Figure 7.7). Have each participant place the color they feel most accurately represents the effect it has.

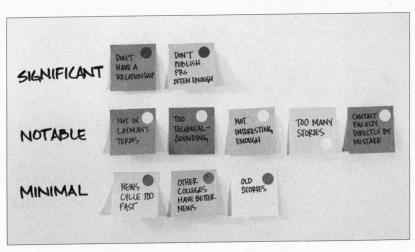

FIGURE 7.7 Characterizing constraints as minimal, notable, or significant.

CONTINUES ➤

CONTINUED ➤

Discuss how the impact of constraints could be removed, or limited, and identify the positive effect of mitigating it as a group. If constraints lead into detailed discussion of a tactic, challenge them with the question "why?" until you get from tactics to strategy.

For example, if the group suggests limiting costs by changing vendors, ask "Why would that limit costs?" If the answer is "the current vendor is too expensive," ask "Why do we know that the current vendor is too expensive?" When the answer to that question is "because the average cost per widget is at least 50% higher than two other competitors," capture the idea.

This may seem a little obvious, but we often throw out ideas based on the assumption that everyone in the room would use similar logic. One person in the room might think that the vendor is reasonably priced, but is taking too much of the overall budget. Anytime you encounter those differences in "why," document them visually as a choice between two competing reasons (see Figure 7.8).

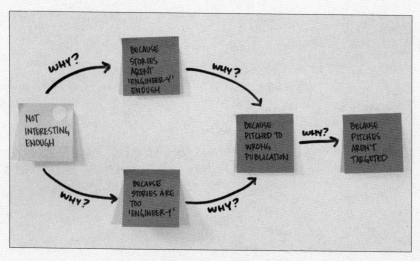

FIGURE 7.8 The results of a "why" chain that demonstrates competing reasons.

After a few "whys," you'll get to a subjective value statement behind the tactics. This is the material on which to build good objectives. Visually document these ideas in increasingly deeper levels vertically on an X axis. Think of it as five layers of "whys," and your goal is to keep diving deeper on each until you get to the connection between the organizational mission and a behavior.

Build Objectives (40 minutes)

The measurable outcome of this meeting is a solid list of objectives that the group agrees are worth pursuing. You've assembled a list of possible attacks to problem constraints, and you've asked a few levels of "why" those attacks would work. This gives you lots of raw material for objectives to browse.

Break the room into smaller groups and assign two or more constraints to each group: one significant constraint, and one or more notable or minimal constraints. Begin with constraints in the minimal or notable category—those will be the easiest from which to form an objective statement. For 20 minutes in small groups, review all the larger group's ideas against that constraint and develop an objective statement that summarizes a changed outcome.

If it helps, refer them to the current key results measures in the initial documentation and ask them to formulate a change in those results as a possible key result that would support an objective. Then each group should build subjective value statements (objectives) that frame why changing those results would matter. Remember, objectives are ambitious but vague. Encourage the group to dream big, and if they get too specific, facilitate them back from the results to the meaning behind those results by probing with "whys."

For the final 20 minutes, share out the final objectives developed by each subgroup and capture them on the wall. Revisit the original problem to begin this conclusive discussion. Dot vote on what objectives they feel have the most potential for affecting desired changes. This will help you leave the meeting with objectives that the group believes are the most promising.

HOW CAN I CONVINCE MY BOSS OR MY CLIENT THAT A WORKSHOP IS WORTH THE TIME AND EXPENSE?

James Macanufo
Creative Director, Pixel Press and coauthor of
Gamestorming

James Macanufo is a facilitation and concept development con-
sultant who cowrote the book Gamestorming *with Dave Gray*
and Sunni Brown. James has facilitated workshops with dozens of Fortune
100 companies, including the U.S. Marine Corps, the U.S. Department of
Education, the Office of the Director of National Intelligence, Intel, IBM,
Hewlett Packard, and many more.

I share skepticism about workshops. I expect everyone has gritted their teeth through at least one expensive, ineffective, poorly prepared, poorly facilitated, wrong place/wrong time affair. Regrettably, I've facilitated a few clunkers myself. Beyond the "just how expensive was that meeting" calculations, I now consider these a waste of real human potential. Time is our only coin, and we ought not take it from each other so eagerly.

With that in mind, a well-run workshop is time well spent.

It's likely that whatever you're working on has no "correct answer" and will require the energy and expertise of a team over a sustained amount of time. A day or more spent up front getting things in order is better than costly cycles of confusion and despair down the road. In this sense, and for the deeply skeptical, a workshop is a risk-mitigating tool.

On the other side of the coin, workshops can be a crucible for new ideas that wouldn't otherwise come to be. Inspiration chooses its own time and place, but a workshop is a chance to create, combine, and test ideas as a group. No emails, no conference calls required—just people working together, listening and learning and creating new things.

Beyond that, a well-run workshop helps people learn how they will work together. Beyond whatever official roles and responsibilities are written down, it's this informal "grease" that ultimately gets things done.

I've learned that people universally want to solve problems and create new things together—just more effectively. Most of the work of a workshop is setting that up and getting out of their way.

I once facilitated a project as a consultant for the Department of Education that came to be known as "School 2.0," before 2.0 was an outdated term. We started with a workshop in Washington DC, which included educators and technologists. Our "straw man concept" was this: let's draw the school of the future.

Quickly, the discussion moved on to explore more interesting concepts. Learning doesn't just happen in the school! It may seem obvious now, but in 2008, it was unconventional to think that teaching and learning happened throughout a community at any time of day.

What worked well during that Department of Education workshop was the bridging of perspectives. When people from different worlds come together to work on something, lateral thinking takes place. They disrupt each other just enough to spark new thoughts. The concept of lateral thinking, coined by Edward de Bono, is loosely this: in problem solving, we're creatures of habit.[5] We run these little loops in our head that tell us we've seen a problem before, so we go from A to B to C, and it's solved. Lateral thinking is breaking those loops, often with randomization to trigger a new perspective. De Bono has techniques to do that intentionally. I think just by bringing people from different backgrounds together, you're forcing some of that to happen.

A group is a little system. They have their interactions, whether they name them or not. They have their habits. One argument is if the system itself is broken, then how do you find the solution within it? If you have six project managers who all have the same problems, what will happen when you get them together to figure out how to do that stuff better? Are they going to come up with new and better ideas or effective ideas? Or would it be more effective to have half as many project managers and a couple of people from other fields? That's lateral thinking, and that's a great reason to have a workshop.

5. Edward de Bono, *Lateral Thinking: Creativity Step by Step* (New York: Harper Perennial, 2015).

Project Kickoff Workshop

You assess a project's success or failure based on how it well it measures against your initial expectations. It's like going to the movies—if you see the latest blockbuster and expect special effects and big action but also get some believable characters, that movie exceeds your expectations. A quiet character drama without believable characters, on the other hand, won't be rescued by the amazing, period-accurate production design. The goal of a project kickoff meeting is to establish expectations that stakeholders and contributors have for a project. It is a daunting task.

But if you skip that meeting, the cost of not capturing and exploring those expectations is more problematic. That cost appears as scope changes, endless iterations, additional sprints, strained working relationships, and lost repeat business. It's better to invest several extra hours at the beginning than hemorrhage hours from the project later.

Goal of Project Kickoff Workshop

A kickoff workshop is different than the quick kickoff meeting discussed earlier in the chapter. It is more robust, produces real work, and takes a lot more effort. A workshop approach to a kickoff needs to capture, categorize, explore, and expand on expectations of all involved. Aligned expectations and clear task boundaries build trust and momentum. To set the stage for that alignment, begin by gathering the expectations. Use the stakeholder interview approach described earlier in this chapter.

Having those interviews in advance of the kickoff meeting is important. Kickoff meetings are a painfully expensive way to capture expectations, because this is essentially a type of research. A big group meeting is a terrible way of doing research. Research itself, via interviews, is a much better tool for research.

You should have one or two team members scout ahead with interviews and other kinds of investigation to catalogue and process expectations into a list. That way, you save everyone the hassle of listening to everything aloud, and the workshop will exceed expectations because you already know what they are. When you establish a track record of exceeding expectations with the first meeting, you're spending less energy getting to know each other, and more energy building trust.

Measuring the Outcomes of a Project Kickoff Workshop

There are two ways to measure how well expectations have been met (or exceeded). The first is by using a priority and feasibility matrix to assign arbitrary numbers to various project goals (see Figure 7.9). This approach documents agreement and ambiguity about project goals identified in the preliminary "scouting" research.

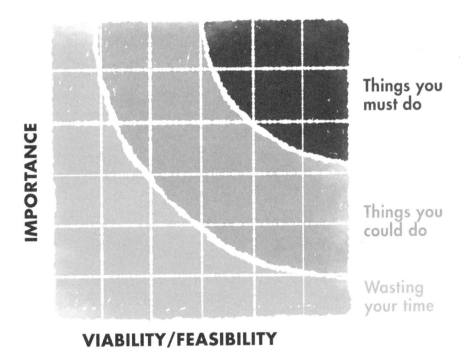

Things you must do

IMPORTANCE

Things you could do

Wasting your time

VIABILITY/FEASIBILITY

FIGURE 7.9 A priority feasibility matrix. The upper right is more "must do," the lower left is more "can drop or skip." The middle is where the most discussion lies.

A second way to measure success is by the presence of new ideas. Those ideas should exist at a sufficient fidelity to obtain approval of the people in charge.

SAMPLE AGENDA FOR A PROJECT KICKOFF WORKSHOP (4–8 HOURS)

A good tool for planning a kickoff agenda is the ARCI matrix.[6] It stands for "accountable, responsible, consulted, and informed." (Some know it as a *RACI* matrix, which is just a shuffle of the same words.) Identify everyone within the organization who has each of these types of relationships with a project. This identifies who should be interviewed prior to the workshop and subsequently invited. Using the sequence A, R, C, and I, reach out to individuals within the company and find each of the following:

- (A's) Accountable people are in leadership positions and make the decisions that guide overall project intentions. These people can sign off on a project decision and decide whether the project has been successful.

- (R's) Responsible people are tied to executing the project's actual work. They are the people making the things that will result in the project being evaluated successfully, or not, by the "accountables."

- (C's) Consulted people have domain expertise that can contribute to a better project. They may not even be on the project team or even in the same company. But their experience or previous research makes their insight relevant to the work at hand. They are the people who can quantify (or qualify) why the project is evaluated as a success.

6. "Organization Charts and Position Descriptions," in *A Guide to the Project Management Body of Knowledge PMBOK Guide*, 5th ed. (Newtown Square, PA: Project Management Institute, 2013), p. 262.

The context of a project kickoff varies with the type of business that you may work in. I'm going to share an agenda for a kickoff workshop to conceive of a new mobile phone application. It's generalized enough, however, that you can apply this agenda workshop structure to whatever kind of project you happen to be kicking off.

- (I's) Informed people are dependent on the project, but may not be responsible for the work or its direction. They are affected by the project's outcome, but do not play a role in it. This inquiry can extend downstream, across the stream, or upstream to dependent direct reports, affected departments, and senior leadership, respectively.

Talk to as many people as you can from each group, but make sure that you connect with the A's and the R's first, and then as many of the C's and I's as you can. Comb the conversation transcripts for precious project expectations. Categorize them using whatever category labels naturally emerge.

For a mobile phone application design project, categories could include brand, art direction, user experience, content strategy, interface design, platform and technology limitations, audience definition, audience acquisition strategy, and back-end technological requirements. Once all expectations are captured and categorized, distribute them to the team that will be attending the kickoff. Each person should apply a number from 1 to 5 for priority (where 5 is high priority) and another number from 1 to 5 for feasibility (where 5 is highly feasible or "easy to do"). Use a web form like this one (see Figure 7.10). Include anyone who seems strongly tied to one of those four categories, but don't organize them as such. In fact, the less expectations are directly related to ARCI roles, the better. This flattens the organization, and ideas should thrive based on merit.

CONTINUES ➤

Sample Priority and Feasibility Form

This is an example of a form used to create a priority and feasibility matrix.

How important is feature or functionality item 1?

        1   2   3   4   5
Low priority ○   ○   ○   ○   ○   High priority

How feasible is feature or functionality item 1?

        1   2   3   4   5
Hard to do ○   ○   ○   ○   ○   Easy to do

How important is feature or functionality item 2?

        1   2   3   4   5
Low priority ○   ○   ○   ○   ○   High priority

How feasible is feature or functionality item 2?

        1   2   3   4   5
Hard to do ○   ○   ○   ○   ○   Easy to do

SUBMIT

FIGURE 7.10 A simple web form can populate a priority feasibility matrix. Score averages and standard deviations, and watch for high standard deviations relative to the range (e.g., 1.5 or greater). This implies disagreement in the expectations of the group.

Introduction (30 minutes)

You've captured everyone's project expectations in advance. Begin by asking what they expect out of the *workshop itself*. A half-day for many people is a huge commitment. Express consideration for people giving up their time to make this gathering possible. Simply ask, "What would you like to accomplish in this workshop?" Have each person speak aloud a short answer. Capture all responses, with names, so that you can return to this list later.

Prioritization and Feasibility Exercise (15 minutes, optional)

You can conduct the prioritization and feasibility analysis in the meeting if you haven't done so in advance using a web form. Hand out a prioritization and feasibility worksheet like the one you saw previously, or have people fill out a web version. Allow everyone a few moments to record their scores. Remind them that the score totals for each of the two categories (priority and feasibility) should be equal to three times the number of questions in that category. Collect the forms and perform some quick calculations—you may want to take a five-minute break to allow for that.

Prioritization and Feasibility Scores (30 minutes)

Briefly review items that averaged lowest in both priority and feasibility. In a visual plot, these items will lie in the lower left (see Figure 7.11). Spend the remaining time reviewing expectations that score in the middle or higher bands, and take special note anytime the priority score or feasibility score for a single expectation has a high standard deviation. High standard deviation indicates conflicting opinions.

For conflicting opinions, identify why something might be important (or perceived as easy) for one party but might be unimportant (or perceived as difficult) for another. Left unexplored, those conflicts will haunt the project. Identify each conflict but do not try to solve each one right away, unless a simple solution presents itself, such as a misunderstanding of the requirements or a lack of technical expertise about the problem.

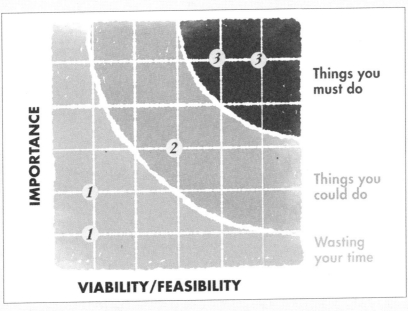

FIGURE 7.11 Plotted areas of low (1), middle (2), and high priority (3).

CONTINUES ➤

CONTINUED ➤

Hypothesis Design Exercise (1 to 2 hours)

No one designs a mobile app just to have a mobile app. There are assumptions about what benefit the app will provide to a business. The same could be said of any project. There's hope that the project will benefit the business, and that benefit should be clarified to establish which project outcomes are desired. The following exercise addresses this, and is based on a worksheet from the book *Lean UX* by Jeff Gothelf and Josh Seiden (see Figure 7.12).[7]

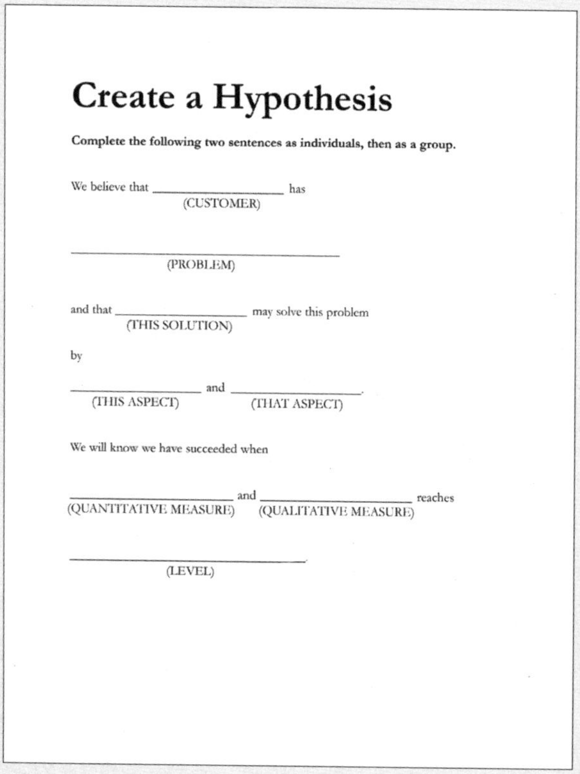

Create a Hypothesis

Complete the following two sentences as individuals, then as a group.

We believe that _____ has
(CUSTOMER)

_____
(PROBLEM)

and that _____ may solve this problem
(THIS SOLUTION)

by

_____ and _____.
(THIS ASPECT)   (THAT ASPECT)

We will know we have succeeded when

_____ and _____ reaches
(QUANTITATIVE MEASURE)   (QUALITATIVE MEASURE)

_____
(LEVEL)

FIGURE 7.12 Use this worksheet to design a hypothesis for your project during a kickoff meeting.

7. Jeff Gothelf and Josh Seiden, *Lean UX* (Sebastopol, CA: O'Reilly Media, 2013).

Distribute the worksheet. Working alone, everyone should fill out their beliefs about the mobile app's audience, the problem they believe the audience has that the app will solve, and the qualitative and quantitative measures of success that they imagine will prove the app has value.

After everyone has filled out their worksheet alone, form groups of two. Those pairs should mix discipline, department, ARCI role, or all the above. Avoid pairing people who already work together regularly or do similar jobs, as they will reinforce each other's assumptions. The more you connect different kinds of people, the more understanding, variation, and value you will get.

Take turns sharing their hypotheses in groups of four; then have the group of four collaboratively develop a new hypothesis. The most compelling ideas should bubble to the top of the discussion. To experiment with results, socially engineer groups so that at the end of the process, you have diverse group composition of job or ARCI roles. Compare and discuss the different group hypotheses.

Once you have arrived at two hypotheses, have Group 1 take ownership of Group 2's hypothesis and vice versa. Then take a break before the next step. Next, you'll conduct a design studio based on the hypothesis each group has been assigned.

Break (15 to 30 minutes)

Remember from Chapter 2, "The Design Constraint of All Meetings," you'll want to take breaks in any workshop every 90 minutes or so, or lose people's interest to devices and other tasks they could be working on.

Design Studio Exercise (90 minutes to 3 hours)

Each group begins with a hypothesis that articulates who the audience is, why they need a mobile app, and how success will be measured. Starting with these hypotheses, go through the same "working alone to working in groups" process. But this time, instead of filling out a madlib worksheet, you'll sketch ideas for the interface or experience of the app itself. Use blank paper or provide sketch sheets that have blank screens on them (see Figure 7.13).

CONTINUES ➤

CONTINUED ➤

Choose a set of project expectations from the priority and feasibility discussion to explore while drawing screens for each hypothesis. Pick ones that scored in compelling ways (high standard deviation or high average priority or feasibility).

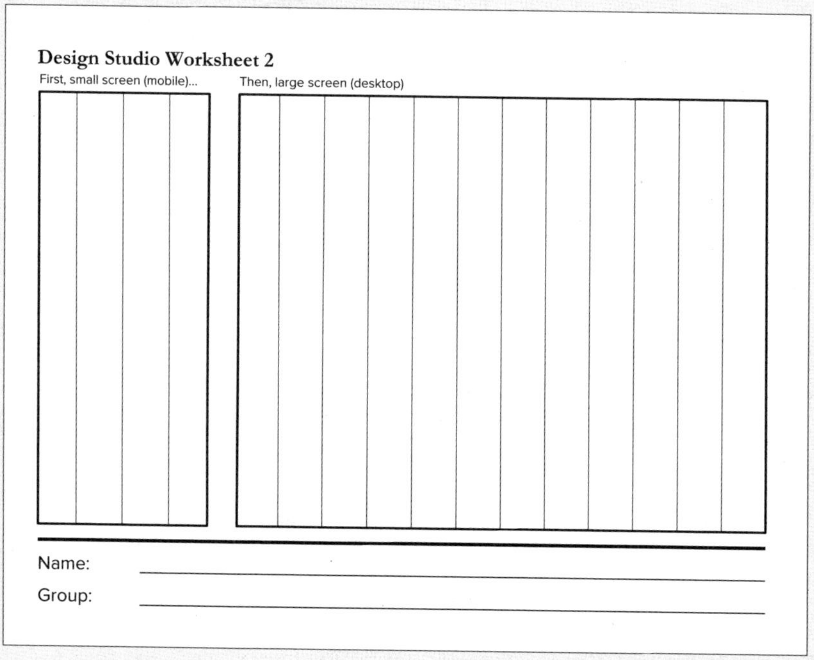

Design Studio Worksheet 2

First, small screen (mobile)...   Then, large screen (desktop)

Name: _____

Group: _____

FIGURE 7.13 Blank design studio sketching sheets for a mobile application.

Maintain tight time limits—this will take time to finish, and working quickly gets the obvious ideas out of the way. Working alone, roughly sketch six or more ideas in 10 minutes and then work on single ideas for 10 to 15 minutes, with the same amount of time to share and critique before sketching. For example, a group of 16 people follow this timing sequence:

- Sketch alone: 10 minutes

- Groups of 2 critique: 10 minutes (5 minutes for each partner to present and discuss)

- Groups of 2 sketch: 15 minutes

- Groups of 4 critique: 15 minutes (7 minutes for each group of 2 to present and discuss)
- Groups of 4 sketch: 15 minutes
- Groups of 8 critique: 20 minutes (10 minutes for each group of 4 to present and discuss)
- Groups of 8 sketch: 20 minutes
- Groups of 8 share: 20 minutes (10 minutes for each group to present and critique)
- Total time: 2 hours and 5 minutes

Extend the time required to accommodate larger groups of people, but don't let any single group exceed eight people, as conversation becomes unwieldy due to the points of agreement model, as discussed in Chapter 3, "Build Agendas Out of Ideas People, and Time."

It can be intimidating to sketch for people who don't normally draw. You'll hear complaints of "I'm not an artist," or "Isn't this what the designers are supposed to be doing?" Reassure the group that this is not meant to result in a design, but in a lot of great conversation about the jobs the design is intended to perform. This exercise reveals critical assumptions and defines the edges of what is possible. If it helps, have the whole group warm up by sketching these simple shapes shown in Figure 7.14, each of which easily translates into a component of a simple interface. This will establish expected fidelity and level the playing field, so that nonsketchers can express their ideas with the artists in the room.

FIGURE 7.14 Simple shapes for the user interface (or anything) that anyone can draw, from Dave Gray and Sunni Brown.

CONTINUES ➤

CONTINUED ➤

When you're a consultant working with a client, challenge expectations. You can try the following variations:

- Have only trained designers sketch while in groups, once you assemble groups. The designers should sketch what the group is describing and not sketch their own contributions. They can add those later.

- Have only nondesigners sketch. It sounds mean, but having the designers do most of the verbal heavy lifting and thinking can really change the conversation dynamic in positive ways. It can play out as a productive role-reversal.

- Sketch only in black permanent marker, forcing people to get it right and keep it simple. You're going to have perfectionists in the group, trying to achieve the Mona Lisa of sketches. That's the wrong idea. Limit their ability to endlessly iterate by erasing erasers.

Sharing Out and the "Golden Tickets" (20 to 30 minutes)

Have each group share their final idea. Spend more time than you have in the past critiquing these final sketches. In a larger group, capture feedback on sketches by having everyone sketch their final idea at a larger scale on a whiteboard. After presenting the final sketch to the group, write down feedback on different color Post-it Notes, using a different color for each question:

- What is the best part of this sketch?

- What will be difficult to do in this sketch?

Once all answers are written down (one answer per note), everyone should post their notes directly on the sketch, and the sketch can be photographed will all its annotated feedback included. Use initials on each note so that if follow-up questions are required, you know who posted what piece of feedback.

For senior stakeholders in the room—the ones who put the "A" in Accountable—provide two or three of a uniquely colored Post-it Note, a color that visually pops out from a distance. Capture any executive decisions they've made within the sketch by writing them down on those "golden tickets." If they see something that is a "must-have" or a "superb idea," they can note what they like, posting it directly on the sketch itself.

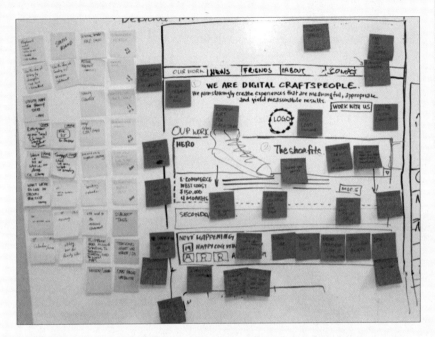

FIGURE 7.15 A critiqued final sketch with a few "golden tickets."

Take Another Break (15 to 30 minutes)

Immediate Next Steps and Action Item Assignments (15 minutes)

Wrap up with immediate next steps that should be taken based on the priorities selected, hypotheses finalized, and sketches critiqued. Quickly draft a clear sequence of events from the work you've done together to expected outcomes. If necessary, explain which party will be executing each task.

Then you might want to have a party or treat the team to a fantastic happy hour or dinner! They've earned it.

WHAT YOU NEED TO KNOW

You may have noticed that there are more agendas in this chapter than any other in Part II of the book. Beginning meetings are where there is the most potential for progress because there is the least alignment. There are different ways to build that alignment, and these agendas provide the most flexibility in starting within different constraints of time, desired outcomes, and organizational culture. Be sure to keep the following things in mind for any meeting at the start of a process.

- Reveal and explore assumptions first. Then build agreement around those assumptions, identify conflicts, and finally pursue decisions. Follow a good conversational pattern.

- Use what you learn in advance meetings, like stakeholder interviews or workshop planning meetings to design a better agenda for the main event.

- When prioritizing or resolving conflicts, fall back on voting methods and consider protocols where you don't have to speak. These methods level the playing field for employees and their bosses, as well as people who contribute in different styles.

- Don't always assume the best person to do something is the person who is already good at that thing. Having someone who isn't very good at drawing a sketch, with a facilitator guiding them, will result in different results than having an experienced artist sketch ideas.

8

Chart the Course Using Middle Meetings

When a team is further into working together on a project, habits transform into "business as usual." The meaning of "usual" depends on the number of people, prior successes, personality types, and many more factors. To get a group of varied personalities and perspectives to stay rallied around an outcome over a long project is hard. Different backgrounds, skill sets, and conflicts will slow things down at best, or at worst will bring them to a complete halt.

But as you know from Chapter 4, "Manage Conflict with Facilitation," working through conflict and discomfort is healthy and necessary. People with good intentions have different facilitation styles and unspoken plans. Those differences contain new and innovative solutions. Meetings can surface useful conflicts in unexpected ways. Getting through the middle of the process—when everyone might not see eye-to-eye—involves exploring the possible to find the most viable way forward.

The middle of a process is about mapping the territory, which is often done on a larger, organizational scale with annual retreats. Retreats are places to reflect on alignment around an organization's mission, to surface conflicts, and to celebrate accomplishments. Smaller scale middle meetings are regular check-in meetings like "stand-ups." But at both ends of the scale, middle meetings are powerful tools for mapping out how an organization might navigate internal or external forces that demand growth or change.

To figure out which end of the scale to focus on, think about the "sight distance" of the conversation. For status meetings and check-ins, it makes sense to limit how far ahead you are looking. Agile development processes with daily check-ins, or "scrums," make sight distance very precise by organizing it around lengths of time, known as "sprints." This ensures that people in a scrum only think about what is in the immediate future. They tend to stay focused on no more than a day to a week's worth of effort. Other "middle meetings," such as presenting results from a study or proposing a design direction, also serve to map territory. They can, however, reorient the map by introducing new constraints, goals, or pathways to pursue. Retreats can vastly alter that territory, reflecting and redefining core aspects of an organization's identity.

Here are several kinds of the most common mid-process and mid-project meetings, with agendas that you can tailor for your unique culture. Each example provides an outcome or goal, how you measure that goal, and a sample agenda. This selection of meetings is not meant to provide an exact sequence to follow: it's an a la carte menu. Look through the different types and select the one that fits your needs based on the sight distance you're expecting to explore. Then tailor it to *your* organization and desired outcomes.

In addition, this chapter introduces some aspects of the traditional, capital "A" Agile process. This book is not meant to be a guide for how to bring Agile (or even agile) methodology into your work. But if you are new to Agile, you can use the concepts in this chapter to experiment with approaches to meetings you have in your variation of Agile methodology. (We'll stick with lowercase "a" agile from here on out.) For more on agile methodology, there are a number of books on the subject, such as *Agile Software Development: Principles, Patterns, and Practices.*[1]

Agile Style Daily Scrum

The daily scrum is the heart of an agile process—it's the meeting you'll have the most often. The name "scrum" is based on the "scrummage:" the part of a rugby game when play restarts after a foul occurs or the ball goes out of bounds. Everyone from each team grabs for the ball huddled together in a circle and then puts their heads together in interlocking fashion. Afterward, play continues from that point. In an agile scrum style meeting, everyone is grabbing for work to undertake.

Goal of an Agile Style Daily Scrum

Hopefully, daily scrum meetings are not as dangerous as a scrummage on the rugby field. But the intention is similar: getting the project back into play from where work last stopped. It usually happens in the morning, and its goal is broadcasting information. A scrum meeting establishes a shared awareness of what everyone on the project completed yesterday, what they are working on today, and what barriers they are encountering in their tasks.

---

1. Robert C. Martin, *Agile Software Development: Principles, Patterns, and Practices* (Upper Saddle River, NJ: Pearson, 2003).

It's not uncommon for people outside a project team, such as senior leadership, to sit in on a daily scrum as a way of checking on progress. But it's not a good idea for those people to contribute to the discussion. Extended analysis is against a scrum's purpose, which is to get a detailed picture of project progress that has happened in the past 24 hours. Further discussions or problem resolution should happen immediately following a scrum, but outside of it, so as to protect the working time of the team.

Measuring the Outcomes of a Daily Scrum

Kanban[2] is a flavor of agile methodology, which uses a "kanban board." The board is a visual tool for capturing the activities reported within a scrum meeting (see Figure 8.1). It's a series of columns in which cards (work activities) can be placed. A basic kanban has three columns (from left to right): items to do, items being done, and items completed. These correspond to the three components of the daily scrum discussion: work identified that hasn't been done yet (column 1); work that is in process (column 2); and work that has been completed (column 3). A productive daily scrum meeting can be measured by the quantity of items that exist on a kanban board, and the overall progress those items are making from the left to the right (see Figure 8.2).

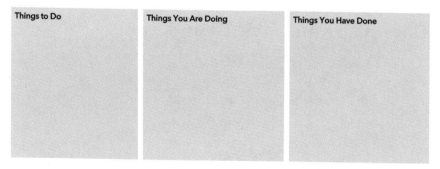

FIGURE 8.1 A blank, basic kanban board. You can label the columns appropriately for your process.

2. Paul Schönsleben, *Integral Logistics Management*, 5th ed. (Boca Raton, FL: CRC Press, 2016), p. 303.

FIGURE 8.2 A kanban-style board can be used to capture discussion during a daily scrum meeting. Move items into the appropriate column, from left to right.

When there are a lot of items added in the first column (to do), you know the scrum is working because work is being identified. When items are moved to the second or third column, the kanban board conveys the active health of the project. Time-lapsed photography of a kanban provides insight into the increases and decreases in work quantity. Tasks that are problematic will get stuck in the middle column, so it's a good idea to include a limit for the center column. This can be based on the number of items assigned to a single person at any given time. For example, "There should never be more than three items assigned to anyone in the center column." These limits are referred to as *work-in-progress limits*, or WIP limits.

Kanbans can be much more complex than three columns. If you're new to the concept, these three columns are a good place to start. More advanced variations on the kanban board might include fully articulated steps in software development. Here's a five-column one that includes steps for backlog and quality assurance testing (see Figure 8.3).

SAMPLE AGENDA FOR AGILE STYLE DAILY SCRUM (ROUGHLY 10 MINUTES, NOT TO EXCEED 8 PEOPLE)

The person who facilitates a daily scrum is called a *scrum master*. That person is tasked with facilitating the movement from scrum to scrum and column to column. There are plenty of articles, books, courses, and certifications out there promising to make you a good scrum master, if that is your role. At a basic level, keep in mind that the scrum master is a manager of tasks, not people.

If you're the scrum master, start the meeting on time, regardless of who is in attendance. One by one, each team member reports the work that they completed yesterday. The scrum master then moves each item to the appropriate column in the kanban board.

Any new assignments that result from completed work are noted by the scrum master for later addition to the kanban board. The scrum master and the team are careful to note any WIP (work-in-progress) limits for the "doing" column.

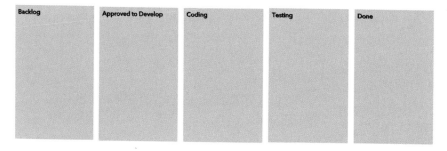

FIGURE 8.3 A more complex kanban board used for development teams.

Each team member reports the work that they intend to undertake today. The scrum master moves the corresponding tasks from "to-do" into "getting done."

Finally, team members share if they feel unable to begin or continue a task due to an unmet dependency. The scrum master notes those dependencies and identifies which team members will need to have further discussion, outside of but immediately following the scrum meeting.

That's it—it may sound simple but it's highly effective at identifying work-flow dependencies inside (and outside) of a team. An effective scrum master will keep the meeting duration to a minimum, as well as remove a few task barriers if possible.

Weekly Project Check-In

If you find agile methodology inflexible, a weekly project check-in might be a better fit. Project check-ins should be brief, tailored to the team, and tailored to the organization. A culture that micromanages will require longer check-ins, more detail, and greater representation at a meeting. A "hands-off" approach will assume that most of the work is proceeding as expected, and they'll have shorter check-ins that focus on major barriers, approvals, and upcoming milestones.

Neither one of these is "the right kind of check-in meeting." Customize your weekly check-in style to suit your group. If people begin complaining that the check-in is a waste of time, consider changing it to better suit the tastes of the organization.

Goal of a Weekly Project Check-In

A check-in meeting broadcasts project communications to the group just like a scrum. Those communications include details about project tasks, upcoming milestones, and delays with their associated causes. It also manages short-term expectations of the team and accountable managers, when those managers are present. They may not need to be present; however, the more often senior stakeholders are present, the more detailed (or derailed) discussions can be.

This has a negative impact on the goal of the meeting because you begin analyzing past project decisions as dictated by a stakeholder's whims. This approach disorients the discussion of day-to-day efforts. Use a parking lot to capture ideas unique to stakeholder awareness and address those ideas in a separate meeting. That parking lot and an occasional stakeholder update meeting reduce confusion arising out of competing team and stakeholder awareness needs being met in a single meeting.

Those additional meetings (and the stakeholder parking lot) will require a designated facilitator. Meetings that beget meetings are the worst, but protecting the team's time by minimizing their exposure to leaderships' goose chases is important. A check-in facilitator keeps the discussion to the appropriate level of detail and keeps it from going over time. The owner of that facilitation role should change from week to week. This avoids the feeling that only "one person" has the true version of events.

Measuring the Outcome of a Weekly Project Check-In

Weekly check-ins serve two masters. On the one hand, they should help a team become more cohesive by reducing dependencies. Finding those dependencies might require going on a few tangents, so letting people go off the reservation a little bit can be a good thing. On the other hand, they are also intended to manage project expectations. People who focus only on outcomes will simply want questions answered about what's coming next. For this reason, it's good to begin the meeting by collecting questions and then measure the meeting's effectiveness by the number of those questions it resolves.

SAMPLE AGENDA FOR WEEKLY PROJECT CHECK-IN (UP TO 30 MINUTES)

Core project team members should be required to attend; otherwise, attendance can be optional. Project managers can designate who is required, based on what they should report each week. Start by making sure that the busiest people are there, because they will be the most engaged in the project work, and therefore the most necessary. For absentees, a summary can be built each meeting, consisting only of actions taken and new action items with assigned parties. Anything that resembles a court transcript will share the same fate that all overwritten meeting notes experience: a quick death, so don't waste time taking these kinds of notes.

Collecting Questions (5 to 10 minutes)

Identify questions that you would like to have answered by the team, but don't pursue answers yet. Give each member of the team a chance to express the questions that they have as well. Collect all questions in one place so that you can sort them quickly into a discussion.

Addressing Questions (5 to 10 minutes)

Start with questions that have simple answers, such as when will this task be done, or why was this task delayed? Capture answers that can be provided quickly. Move on to the more difficult questions, being careful to move any overly detailed dependencies into a parking lot for later.

Upcoming Milestones (5 to 10 minutes)

Identify the next major project efforts and who will undertake each effort. If there are deliverables or accomplishments in the next two weeks of work, identify them and note any feedback cycles or approvals that could impede progress and how long the impact might be. Keep a list of those deliverables handy, either on the wall or in your notes, for revisiting them as questions (e.g., "Where are we on this?") at the beginning of the next weekly meeting.

"Lean Coffee" Check-In

A "lean coffee" can serve as a variation on a check-in meeting that is well suited for emergent priorities and flexible discussion. Jim Benson and Jeremy Lightsmith originally applied this approach in a local meet-up for discussing challenges in applying lean (a type of agile) methodologies in different company cultures.[3]

Attendance is open, inconsistent, and can scale to a larger number if needed. Lean coffees work well even if you don't have the same people attending each meeting. It's a good fit for groups that don't meet regularly but need to coordinate a project or discussion over a long time. Coffee isn't required, but it couldn't hurt (ever).

Goal of a Lean Coffee

This meeting's goal is twofold. First, the group's priorities drive the discussion, and second, task assignments are built based on those priorities. Group members should take ownership of tasks as they are identified. As the group changes from meeting to meeting, so do those tasks and priorities. If the meeting is openly documented, lesser priorities can be identified, assigned, and set aside for future efforts when time and resources allow.

Measuring Outcomes of a Lean Coffee

A lean coffee visually organizes the discussion. It's like a kanban board but less structurally rigid. Cards or Post-it Notes are used to raise and capture interest in issues (see Figures 8.4 and 8.5).

---

3. Jim Benson and Jeremy Lightsmith, http://leancoffee.org

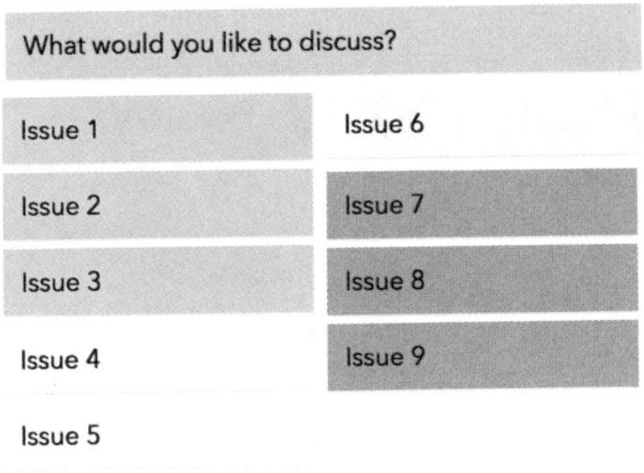

FIGURE 8.4 Lean Coffee Step 1: Add new issues.

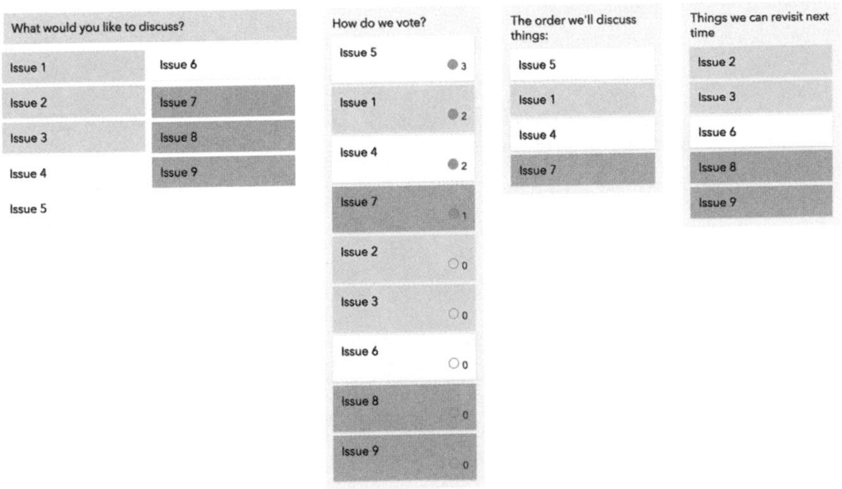

FIGURE 8.5 Lean Coffee Step 2: Vote on issues and then discuss.

Success in each individual meeting is measured by the total number of topics/cards added (quantity) and the interest attendees have within those topics/cards (quality). Better lean coffees have a greater quantity of topics and votes more localized within a smaller set of topics. Success can be measured across multiple meetings by how many raised topics are retired from future meetings. When the same topics come up over and over, the meeting may not be doing the job for which it's intended.

SAMPLE AGENDA FOR LEAN COFFEE (30 MINUTES TO 1 HOUR)

Use the same board each time you meet. Track the emergence and progress for various points of discussion, and refer to previous discussions as group memory, instead of relying on your own occasionally faulty memory.

Capture Topics (up to 10 minutes, depending on size of group)

Working alone, each person lists out topics they would like to discuss. Each topic is written on a single card or Post-it Note in plain language. Encourage people to write in such a way that they could read the card out of the context of previous meetings and still have an idea of what it means. Peruse the board for previous topics that anyone would like to raise again and create new cards for topics being reintroduced. Move those into the current discussion for a voting round.

Vote on Topics (up to 5 minutes)

Allot a certain number of dot votes to each person in attendance. For most size groups, three votes should be sufficient, but five votes might be good for smaller gatherings (fewer than 10 people). Each attendee distributes their votes to the topics by placing a single dot (marker or dot sticker) on the things that they would like to cover. They can place more than one dot on a card/topic about which they feel strongly; they can even put all their votes in a single topic. By being flexible about the distribution of votes, stronger feelings can be accommodated.

Discuss Topics (15 to 45 minutes)

Sequence the discussion based on the number of votes. Discuss topics that have the most votes first, followed by topics that have fewer votes. Topics that have no votes can be cast aside or saved for future gatherings. It's OK to let go of some things—for example, if someone raised a topic but didn't vote for it, they must have felt that other topics were more important.

This discussion should be *lightly* facilitated. The larger the group, the less light the facilitation will be. Very large groups may merit having smaller group discussions and breakout sessions devoted to topics based on votes: everyone who voted for topic A, join group A, etc.

Presentations (of Deliverables, Findings, or Concepts)

The passage of time in our work is often marked with deliverables. They take the form of research reports, slide decks, design comps, conceptual strategic documents, requirements lists, and many more. Some deliverables should be read, and some should be seen with an accompanying speaker, but most combine the writing with visuals. Deliverables are intended to simplify learning something complex, or consolidate complex topics down to portable and memorable concepts.

Goal of a Presentation

The goal of a presentation is getting feedback, approval, or both. If the audience includes the team that did the work, it's more likely to be feedback in the form of a critique. Critical discussions of work (critiques) are covered later in this chapter.

When presenting your ideas to stakeholders, the goal is approval. There may be choices related to approval, such as choosing between multiple recommendations.

> *It's equally (if not more) important to be able to read the room as it is to prepare a compelling presentation.*
>
> **—ALISON BEATTIE**
> **DIRECTOR OF USER EXPERIENCE, TARGET**

If you can't convince your audience that your work is valuable by the time the meeting is over, one of two problems exist. The first is that the meeting was premature, and the work wasn't done yet. If that isn't the case and the work is sound, then the second is that the presentation wasn't convincing. This approach will help you with the latter problem.

Measuring Outcomes of a Deliverable Presentation

This meeting either results in an approval or a response of "get back to work." There are shades of gray between these two outcomes. Depending on how a process or an organization is structured, the meeting's purpose

---

SAMPLE AGENDA FOR A DELIVERABLE PRESENTATION (30 MINUTES TO 1 HOUR)

Do not read the deliverable during the presentation. *Do not read the deliverable during the presentation.* Lest you think a copy editor isn't doing their job, I meant to say that twice, and I'll say it again: if you are reading a deliverable to your audience in a presentation, you are doing the audience and yourself a disservice. To your audience, you are saying, "I'm sure you didn't take the time to look at this before you came, so let me read it to you." If they didn't look at it before the meeting, shame on them! That's not what the meeting should be about.

A presentation shouldn't be where your audience learns about the work for the first time. It should be where your audience processes the implications of the work. You are doing *yourself* a disservice because you are saying, "I don't care enough about my (our) work to explain why it is important. I'll leave that to you to figure out." Rather than reading a deliverable during the presentation, try the agenda that follows. There is a shorter and a longer approach.

Capture Questions (5 to 10 minutes)

The deliverable has been distributed in advance of the meeting (ideally at least two full work days), so there's a good chance that people are going to be coming to the meeting with questions. Ask people to share their questions aloud at the beginning of the meeting. Write down the questions,

---

may be to present directly to decision-makers, to prepare an executive team to present to decision-makers, or to collect feedback and approve the work democratically in a vote. In each case, success is measured by calculating the distance you've moved from where you were before the presentation to where you are at the presentation's conclusion. The goal is to make progress toward a final approval.

noting who asked them. Allow each person to ask the same number of questions and encourage them to keep it brief and direct. Don't answer the questions just yet. Just start by capturing them so that they are collected and visible to everyone.

Short Agenda: Just Answer the Questions (15 to 20 minutes)

If the questions are straightforward, time is limited, and you're good at thinking on your feet, structure your presentation to answer these questions. Re-sequence any prepared material to touch on each one in a logical order, checking them off as you go. An example of a logical order would be to start with the simple questions first and then move on to the more complex ones.

> You (shouldn't) be invited or even allowed to attend the research findings presentation if you haven't observed at least one, ideally two, research (usability testing, user interview, etc.) sessions.
>
> **—DANA CHISNELL**
> **CODIRECTOR, CENTER FOR CIVIC DESIGN**

CONTINUES ➤

CONTINUED ➤

Long Agenda Part I: Present Stories (20 to 40 minutes)

Prepare stories about the work based on what you've learned while making the deliverable. A basic story has a beginning that establishes a context, a middle that presents a conflict, and an ending that results in a degree of resolution. Develop two or three stories based on the content within the deliverable.

For example, present a research report by telling the story of the findings. What environment do the findings reveal? Where is the conflict in that environment? How do the findings resolve that conflict? If it's a design concept, what do we know that makes the concept a good idea? Where do different users of a design encounter challenges? How does the design address their challenges? Each story should take about five minutes, and it should touch on critical elements in the deliverable. Build stories that spotlight the most interesting aspects of the work, such as tough choices that were made, surprises discovered, and the most compelling problems solved.

Long Agenda Part II: Revisit Questions (10 to 20 minutes)

After stories that put the work into context, return to the questions that you captured in the beginning. Answer as many of them as you can. Start with the simple ones and revisit or expand on anything you've already said that addressed them. Check with the person who asked the question after each answer, to find out if the answer was sufficient, and if the answer raised additional concerns. Capture those new concerns as questions. It's a *good* thing to leave a presentation with more questions. If you know there's more work to do to get approval, any clarification is progress.

Critiques

A critique is an awkward conversation. If you're *seeking* a critique, it puts you in a very vulnerable place. It's difficult to hear what's wrong with your work. However, if you're *providing* a critique, you may have spent less time with the work and be reacting to your instincts, without a structured goal for what the feedback is supposed to accomplish. The more a critique's goal is structured, the less painful and more productive that time will be.

Goal of a Critique

Some people believe that a brutal critique is better for helping someone learn the difference between good work and bad work. If this is true, making brutal messages less painful might be the desired outcome. But there's more to critiquing effectively than just getting better at your job.

A critique is a single conversation in a longer relationship between an employee and the people who must approve and use their work—clients, bosses, and users. An ongoing, productive relationship among these parties is the long-term benefit of good critiques. A stronger relationship makes it easier for negative conversations to be heard and reach the desired outcome.

Successful critiques help both parties learn more about the context in which work is meant to thrive. To do this successfully, a critique needs to focus on actionable problems that you can do something about. Too often, critiquing parties jump to suggesting solutions. Instead, try to avoid giving solutions in critiques. Doing that prevents the discussion from reaching a fuller understanding of what the problem is and why it matters.

Measuring Outcomes in Critiques

A list of actionable problems with the current state (of the design, of the report, or whatever) is the goal of this meeting. Count these problems and prioritize them. Prioritization makes it possible for the receiving party to put more thought and effort into the right problems.

SAMPLE AGENDA FOR A SCREEN DESIGN CRITIQUE (2 TO 4 HOURS)

A group critique of design work requires a facilitator with an expertise in design. A critique facilitator elicits sufficient detail on each possible problem, as well as the rationale behind why it is a problem. For a website, you should frame the flow of the conversation around a user's journey through the interface. Walk through the user's steps in the process, and along the way, identify ambiguity or roadblocks.

Screen-by-Screen Walkthrough (15 to 30 minutes)

Start by presenting user goals and then briefly discuss any context in which the users might find themselves. This might include the device they are using or environmental factors around them while using it. Then touch on each screen in the user's journey using an enlarged visual, either projected or printed with a plotter-sized printer on large sheets of paper. Everyone should be able to see all the screens from anywhere in the room. If this isn't possible—let's say you're projecting one screen at a time—make it easy to jump back and forth between projections in your prepared slide deck using shortcuts or something similar.

Screen-by-Screen Critique (10 to 20 minutes per screen)

After running through the entire flow, start by walking through the first screen. Give everyone three different colored Post-it Notes to answer the following questions, one answer per note, one color per question type:

- What cannot be changed on this screen? (Color 1)
- What could be improved on this screen? (Color 2)
- What could be eliminated from this screen? (Color 3)

Without discussion, have everyone post answers directly onto the projection or printed screen (see Figure 8.6). After the answers are posted, the facilitator can consolidate repeated answers and review what was posted to the group, probing by asking "why" for each question posted. Asking "why" gets people to move away from the details of the execution and toward the actionable problem.

Push further than a single "why" when necessary. Capture a list of the actual problems that arise in discussion by screen. Collect them throughout the meeting on a separate, visible list, such as a whiteboard or a large Post-it easel.

FIGURE 8.6 Using Post-it Notes to conduct a web design critique.

Review and Prioritization of Problems (15 to 30 minutes)

After you've got a list of the problems, discuss the relative importance of each problem. Start with the most serious and the least serious problems. Then focus on the remaining problems, pushing for agreement about which problems to prioritize. If necessary, conduct a dot-voting exercise. In the end, sequence the effort to solve those problems by starting with problems that have more dots.

This is one way to plan your critique. You can also decide when you need a critique, or any meeting in a project, by "thinking backward" into well-designed middle meetings. Adam Connor explains how to think backward by helping you develop a rationale for the meetings that you need, rather than coming up with agendas for the meetings that you already have.

WHAT MEETINGS DO YOU NEED?

Adam Connor

VP Organizational Design and Training, Mad*Pow and coauthor of *Discussing Design*

Adam Connor is a western Massachusetts-based designer, author, and illustrator. As the lead for Mad*Pow's Organizational Design practice, he focuses his design skills on helping organizations build teams, processes, and structures that allow them to be creative, collaborative, and productive.

The tension in the room was so thick it was nearly visible. It was just myself, my teammates, and a few project stakeholders present. The rest of the workshop's participants had all left when we ended the session about 15 minutes earlier. We'd hung back to discuss the next steps, and it had just become very clear that where the workshop had left us was not nearly as far along as we needed to be.

The client had pulled strings and nudged people here and there to make sure that everyone showed up, and we had just taken up a full day of their time and energy. The expectation had been that coming out of the workshop we'd have nailed down an idea that could be quickly proto-typed to test with users. We weren't even close to that point.

Remembering that workshop still makes me cringe. It was early in my career. It was one of the first times I'd ever led a project, and to be honest I'm shocked anyone let me do it again after that. But since then I've learned a lot about what it takes to bring people together to work on a problem effectively and efficiently, and a big part of that is working backward from outcomes to meetings. Working this way has become core to how I work and something I find myself talking about with designers and organizations all the time as they run into challenges like mine.

What It Means to Work Backward

At the end of a workshop or meeting, you can find yourself in a place other than where you'd hoped to be. Maybe sometimes you feel like you need a workshop to make up the gap, but you know that's unlikely due to the scheduling challenges that arise when trying to get lots of people together. Or maybe you've been faced with planning an upcoming workshop and haven't been sure what activities and topics to include in it. Over the years, to address these challenges and fears, I've built up a habit of working backward when planning workshops and project phases in general.

I begin by trying to pinpoint the actions that the team needs to be able to do immediately following the workshop. To make sure I'm not just following my own perspective, I confirm these actions with the rest of the team and client. Going into a workshop with people having different expectations of the objective is a great way to make sure that things go poorly.

I then ask myself what information or answers the team needs from the workshop in order to take those actions. After I identify the information needed, I can then ask the question again and repeat the process until I create a chain of information requisites all the way back to whatever information and decisions I have so far in the project.

Working Backward for That Unproductive Workshop

In the workshop I described earlier, I should have known that the action to be taken after the workshop was to prototype something for use in a usability study. This would have told me that the workshop needed to end with the team having a clear direction and some detailed interface design. Specifically, what was needed was a set of use-case/interaction flows that we would examine in the studies. From there, the chain of requisite information would flow like this:

- To have a clear direction and establish detailed designs, the team would need to examine, discuss, and choose from interface ideas.

- To examine, discuss, and choose from interface ideas we'd have to generate a variety of ideas for the use cases we were interested in exploring.

- To generate interface ideas for certain use cases, we'd need to look at the potential use cases and prioritize which ones were most important to explore.

CONTINUES ➤

CONTINUED ➤

This process provides a gap analysis between where the team is currently and where it wants to be after our meeting or meetings. With the chain in front of me, I can select the right activities to produce the information, decisions, etc. that we need at each step.

This approach to planning workshops (or sanity-checking existing ones) has saved me a lot of headaches and helped me resolve awkward situations when I need to adjust unrealistic client expectations. Design is all about creating things to achieve specific objectives. When designing your meetings and workshops, starting with objectives and following the flow of requisite information is a great place to start.

Design a Workshop (for Anything)

Workshop design is both simple and complex. The basics are simple: using meeting design principles, such as scaling into groups, designing good questions, and selecting an appropriate facilitation style are a good place to start. Any discussion topic or activity can be turned into a group workshop by applying these principles and following a natural conversation pattern of divergence and convergence.

There are plenty of books filled with good workshop agendas. *Gamestorming* by Gray, Macanufo, and Brown, visual workshop books by David Sibbet,[4] and many more are listed at the end of this chapter. But you don't need to follow a step-by-step recipe to have a good workshop. Here's a structure to build your own workshop approach, which starts by acknowledging the challenge that you'd like to overcome.

---

4. David Sibbet, *Visual Teams* (Hoboken, NJ: Wiley, 2011); David Sibbet, *Visual Leaders* (Hoboken, NJ: Wiley, 2012); David Sibbet, *Visual Meetings* (Hoboken, NJ: Wiley, 2010).

Goal of Any Workshop

James Macanufo articulated good goals for workshops in the previous chapter: to manage long-term risk while creating ideas not possible without mixing diverse perspectives. A good workshop, therefore, allows risks and blends perspectives. Another goal is making decisions. The decisions made in a workshop can be binary and simple—"Should we do something or not?" Or more complex—"How much effort should we apply, who will be assigned to that effort, and when will it be completed?"

Measuring the Outcomes of Any Workshop

Measuring a workshop's outcomes also ranges from simple to complex. You can simply say a decision was made (or not). But a more complex decision will have more complex measurements. Evidence of complex decision-making can be found anecdotally when you can say, "I would have a hard time crediting the workshop outcome to just one person." When one participant dominates the conversation, it doesn't reflect a blended perspective.

Try to keep an eye on the amount of time each person spends saying things, making things, and listening to others. A perfect balance across these three activities is impossible, but it is something to facilitate. Some conference call services even provide a percentage of time speaking for each participant.

"Time boxing," or creating artificial time limits for contributions, are another way to manage the blend of voices in a workshop. This applies to both individuals and groups. Give a group a time limit, and you'll find that they get the obvious out of the way, and then move on to that desired risk-taking.

SAMPLE WORKSHOP DESIGN TEMPLATE (2 HOURS TO 2 DAYS)

Identify a framing question in advance to ask people what they want out of that workshop. For example, what is our current business model, and what are better business models? List the decisions you are trying to make and identify varied perspectives that you can bring to the table as attendees using the ARCI model from Chapter 7, "Get Started with Beginning Meetings." There's no point in holding a workshop with a bunch of similarly minded people.

> *The worst way to set a tone for collaboration during a workshop is by beginning with a presentation, where people don't get to speak. Ask people what they want out of the meeting and let them speak with each other at the beginning to establish that participation is expected and it matters.*
>
> **—JAMES BOX**
> **DIRECTOR OF USER EXPERIENCE, CLEARLEFT LTD**

After you have a list of decisions and a list of people, think about an interesting way to frame the problem that forces everyone to spend time in each of the following conceptual spaces in this sequence, using activities for each of these five spaces that suit the culture of your group and the problem being explored.

1. **Creating workshop tone (30 minutes to 1 hour)**

   How they feel about the problem. Is it important? Is it the wrong problem? If it is wrong, what is the right problem?

2. **Establishing motivation** (**30 minutes to 2 hours**)

Who is motivated to solve the problem? What motivates them? Spend time getting to know the audience in question. Who is served by making these decisions? Who incurs a cost?

3. **Finding answers** (**1 hour to 3+ hours**)

What are all the possible ways to solve the problem? How is it currently being solved? Why is it currently solved the way it is?

4. **Future implications and further conversations** (**30 minutes to 1 hour**)

Explore the deeper meaning of the problem. Your workshop may turn out to be exploring a symptom for deeper, more complex challenges. What are those issues? What are the relationships between the root causes and the problem being examined? This may lead you to dive back into "finding answers" and that's OK. Just make sure to make time to close on the last agenda item.

5. **Making Decisions** (**1 hour to 2 hours**)

As a group, use a voting or input gathering mechanism to finalize and capture decisions. Use dot voting, or ask people to choose one item to save and one item to eliminate. Those decisions could represent project or organizational goals, steps and ownership of tasks, or whatever you like. Just make sure that the decisions are clearly documented so that they make sense out of the context of the conversation.

WHAT YOU NEED TO KNOW

These agendas and agenda structuring methods provide ways to maintain project momentum and put conflict to work. The middle meetings can be some of the toughest, but they're also some of the most important. In a study performed by the National Institutes of Health, the presence of simple, weekly check-in meetings was found to be directly linked to teams that succeeded in solving complex problems.[5] Teams that didn't have regular middle meetings had more trouble in getting work done.

- Middle meetings help you cement a shared vision of work and build trust.

- Trust is necessary to examine the unanticipated challenges that will always arise.

- Middle meetings provide important insight into the assumptions that drive your working relationships.

- You want those relationships to be effective in the long term, beyond the experience of a single meeting.

5. L. Michelle Bennett and Howard Gadlin, "Collaboration and Team Science: From Theory to Practice," *Journal of Investigative Medicine* 60, no. 5 (2012): 768–775. doi: 10.2310/JIM.0b013e318250871d.

9

Find Closure with End Meetings

Bad endings can become good beginnings when you take the time to reflect on what you've done. Insights into how to make the next effort more efficient and fulfilling can be discovered in discussions about where the work ended and why it ended up that way. But finding those insights can be tricky.

Taking an honest look at what happened requires identifying spots where you might have been able to do things better. It means sharing that you've made a few mistakes. Admitting that you've made mistakes in front of other people feels like making yourself vulnerable to attack in a competitive workplace. But like Etsy does with its blameless postmortems (see Chapter 6, "Better Meetings Lead to Better Organizations"), you can design a meeting to focus on problem-solving in place of finger-pointing.

Fear of being blamed is one of the reasons that ending meetings are avoided. Fear of being evaluated negatively is a valid concern. On the other hand, when a team is happy to be done with a good project, opening wounds feels like moving backward. But without looking back, past mistakes repeat themselves.

Here are a few of the most common end meetings, with agendas that you can change to meet your needs. Reviewing final quality assurance test results, postmortems, and retrospectives are different ways to conclude work. While the first influences the final output of a project, the focus of the other two becomes subsequent, future efforts. As in the two previous chapters, each meeting has a goal, a way to measure it, and a starter agenda. These meetings are presented in no particular order. You won't need all of them. Instead, find the one that feels right and change it to suit your needs.

User Acceptance Testing (UAT) Defect Log Reviews

User acceptance testing is a methodology for identifying and addressing bugs within software development projects. It takes place between the completion of software development and the launch of software. The final effort of a UAT process is focused on building observed problems into a list called the *defect log*. The log contains bugs identified in testing, the bugs' relative severity (e.g., high, medium, low), descriptions of what created the problem, and the dates the bug was reported and fixed.

A completed defect log would consist of all fixed items. A series of check-in style meetings where the team assembles to review what defects have been addressed, moving toward the elimination of all bugs, is not uncommon. But honestly, this seems relatively straightforward without the need for developers and software test analysts to meet. What value does a meeting add to this process?

Goal of a UAT Defect Log Review

The goal of any software project is to launch something for users that is error free and works well. The meeting's goal should be to articulate what is left that isn't working well and assign responsibility to address each issue to appropriate individuals or teams before the release of the software.

But there are gray areas when it comes to defining what "works well" means. You could design a perfectly functional way to register for an event, where no step in the process produces an actual error, but it is confusing or tedious because it takes far too many steps, or things are labeled ambiguously. A meeting builds alignment about this meaning.

In addition, discussing a defect log with a mix of developers and non-developers risks scope creep. People will define "wrong" differently, so a good place to start is to revisit the intention of the testing. Is the goal to eliminate faulty code? Are you trying to improve the overall experience of using the design? Or both? Stating the testing intentions at the beginning of the meeting will prevent tangents that don't align well with those intentions. This helps more people have a shared definition of what constitutes "wrong."

Valid problems outside of testing intentions shouldn't be ignored, however. These kinds of problems are labeled as "deferred," which is another way of building a parking lot. The goal of a final defect log review then becomes more complex. First, identify what will be addressed and by whom. Second, find ways to capture the rationale for what is being deferred and how (and when) deferred items will be addressed. A good series of UAT meetings can define the future roadmap of a software development effort, closing the iterative design loop.

Measuring Outcomes of a UAT Defect Log Review

There are two lists maintained in a series of defect log review meetings. The first list is made of the software defects identified at the start of each review. As the development team resolves defects, the number of defects on the list should get smaller between each UAT defect log meeting that takes place, eventually reaching zero. If the number isn't being reduced, the meeting isn't doing a good job of conveying accountability.

SAMPLE AGENDA FOR A UAT DEFECT LOG REVIEW (20 MINUTES TO 1 HOUR)

A defect log is a well-structured and (hopefully) finite list, which can be visualized on a large grid—for example, a spreadsheet or whiteboard (see Figure 9.1). Rows represent the individual defects, and columns represent each of the data points: date identified, severity, description, and so forth. Rather than sending out printed agendas for each meeting, have a large visual representation of the log that is used from meeting to meeting. A photo of the log at the beginning and end of the meeting will demonstrate the changes in bug status or that additional bugs have been added to the log.

Bug	Severity	Status	Date Reported	Reported by	Description/Notes
Software bug title	High, Medium, or Low	Open, Closed, or Deferred	March 31, 2017	Firstname Lastname	Any additional notes you need
Login fails	High	Open	April 2, 2017	Brann	Script times out
List doesn't render	Medium	Open	April 1, 2017	Brent	Ajax spinner keeps spinning
Margins off	Low	Closed	March 15, 2017	Troy	Margins are too large on the home page, second paragraph
File upload corrupts file	Low	Deferred	April 5, 2017	Bill	File upload corrupts file in sandbox, not for current version

FIGURE 9.1 A visual UAT defect log used for discussion. Conduct each UAT meeting around this kind of diagram.

Review Testing Intentions (5 minutes)

Photograph the current state of the log before you begin the meeting. Restate the intention of the testing and provide examples of what a bug

The second list is the number of deferred items. That list should be kept to a minimum and be well documented. The longer each list is, the better the defect log meeting will be. A good defect log review will build each of those lists as much as necessary: first, the complex defects that have not yet been addressed, and second, the defects that are good candidates for deferral.

looks like and what a bug doesn't look like. Check for any questions from the team, especially if they've identified defects that may not meet the testing intentions. Capture those defects as new candidates on the visual log.

Update Existing Defect Statuses (20 to 50 minutes)

Survey the room of developers for bug status updates, including newly identified bugs, and change existing bugs or add new ones. This is a living, breathing visual agenda, so writing on an erasable whiteboard or using removable sticky notes is essential. You'll move things around, replace text, and add or remove content frequently.

The discussion can be facilitated in one of two ways. The first approach has each analyst/tester list all their new bugs or status changes, and then gives developers a chance to ask questions after each bug. An alternative, more engaging flow has each analyst report a single new bug or updated bug status, have developers and other analysts respond and explore, and then move on to another analyst. Changing the party who is reporting the bug as often as possible prevents the team from narrowing the focus. Also, it prevents the monotony of having too much of any single voice.

To review, the recommended flow is as follows:

1. Analyst 1: Reports their Defect 1.
2. Developers and analysts discuss Defect 1.
3. Defect is either assigned or deferred.

CONTINUES ➤

CONTINUED ➤

4. If deferred, it is discussed in the context of previous deferrals.

5. Analyst 2: Reports their Defect 1.

6. Developers and analysts discuss Defect 1.

Continue to cycle through all analysts, eventually starting back with analyst 1 through the cycle again until each person has reported and discussed all bugs.

Review Final Decisions and Capture the Updated Log State (5 minutes)

Revisit each deferral. As a facilitator, be sure to reflect the group's discussion that leads to the deferral. Identify responsible parties for each defect, beginning with the most severe and moving through the less severe deferrals. After the group concurs that everything is done, be sure to photograph and distribute the new state of the UAT board.

Agile Style Retrospectives

Agile methodology uses an end meeting, called a *retrospective*, to conclude the sprint process. Like other agile meetings, retrospectives have a recipe with the intention baked in. As a team becomes more comfortable with each other, they are likely to put their own spin on that recipe.

Agile retrospectives are short meetings in which people sort their learnings from the previous sprint into three categories: new approaches they'd like to take; things to continue doing; and things to discontinue doing. This example of a retrospective, or "retro" for short, will cover the basics of running one. I suggest reading Derby and Larsen's *Agile Retrospectives: Making Good Teams Great* for keeping a retro meeting interesting by getting creative.[1]

---

1. Esther Derby and Diana Larsen, *Agile Retrospectives: Making Good Teams Great* (Dallas: Pragmatic Bookshelf, 2006).

Retrospectives close the loop on the process of iterative improvement agile promises. They help a team self-educate and evolve. Over multiple sprints, retros increase a group's capacity to grow and make positive change in the product or process they manage.

Goal of Agile Style Retrospectives

A retrospective should support team growth. A struggling team uses them to understand each other better, identify gaps in their process, and find better ways of working. When a team is working well, retros document successes so that those successes can be repeated. They also explore opportunities to expand scope and develop new ideas to test in future iterations.

Measuring the Outcome of an Agile Style Retrospective

You can measure a retro by tying it back to the previous retro. Over multiple sprints, effective changes in process should be indicated by a specific metric that is tracked in the subsequent sprint. If you identify a new approach to work in a previous retro, you can measure gains for the current sprint by dividing the new outcome by the previously discussed desired outcome.

Here's an example. A previous retro concludes that redesigning the sign-on process for a mobile app should result in eliminating half of all sign-in failures. If the goal is to reduce it by 50%, and during the sprint it is reduced by 40%, dividing 40 by 50 tells you that the change identified in the previous retrospective was 80% effective. This lack of subjectivity is one of the great things about agile approaches. There's little question whether or not ideas developed in previous retros were any good. Effective retros result in sprints that meet or exceed targets, while ineffective ones don't.

Postmortems

Postmortems allow a team to evaluate if they've done a good job on a project. Traditionally, they are longer than agile style retrospectives, and they can take many forms. They have a reputation for being unappealing and difficult for three reasons.

First, a postmortem is odd because it cannot change the project being discussed, unlike the intent of a retro. Like its namesake, it's an examination of something that has already passed. Second, postmortems have

Discuss Team/System Changes (10 to 20 minutes)

Continue an ideation and reflection loop by going back to writing. Have everyone write each change they'd like to make in the team's approach to the work on a sticky note. Instead of immediately associating metrics while working alone, everyone should share the changes with some rationale for why they want to make the change and discuss possible metrics for each one as a group. You may need to brainstorm more than one metric for each change. System-wide or team-wide changes will have multiple measurements. Explore them all, but settle on one metric as a key performance indicator (for each change) that suits everyone. If necessary, use dot voting to resolve conflicts.

Celebrate Successes and Check Expectations (10 minutes)

Go back and share each change, both individual or team-wide, that met or exceeded a goal from the previous sprint's retro. If you're facilitating the retrospective, encourage other people to weigh in on why those goals were exceeded. It may be because the change was a good idea, or alternatively, because the goal was too easy. If that's a possibility, discuss if the goal should be tougher. Wrap up by spotlighting good work that made successful parts of the sprint possible.

no obvious dependencies. Nothing in a project is waiting for the postmortem to happen. New projects can begin without previous ones being discussed, so there isn't incentive to schedule this meeting. Third, unproductive blame is common in postmortems, which is no fun for anyone.

Despite these challenges, a frank discussion about what's in the rearview mirror can have positive results. A team that has regular postmortems can more easily understand, experiment with, and improve their workflow. This conversation helps you anticipate and address familiar problems more effectively when they arise. By spending time returning to difficult parts of a process, it builds more realistic understanding among team members about future constraints. Nothing builds trust like taking a hard look at what you've done together, wins, warts, wars, and all.

Goal of a Postmortem

A postmortem should uncover anything about the past that informs the future. For that reason, the agenda should spend a greater amount of time on the future than the past. Although it's tempting to do a play-by-play from memory, it will likely result in blame. A focus on the future gives this meeting the job of answering "how can we evolve?" It helps you avoid just exploring the negatives. Getting that sweet mix of future and past, as well as positive and negative, is the facilitator's job.

Measuring Outcomes from a Postmortem

A good postmortem produces actionable insights. If you or your teammates can't act on what you've learned, then it isn't a good use of time. There are several ways to count these insights, but the easiest is to maintain both personal and group lists of possible improvements as a shared visual during the conversation.

That list is a bar chart that proves the value of the meeting. Someone who hasn't yet identified one thing they might do differently should be probed to reflect further. A facilitator should seek out possible improvements across each member of the team during this meeting, and not just focus on people perceived as directly related to project problems (see Figure 9.2).

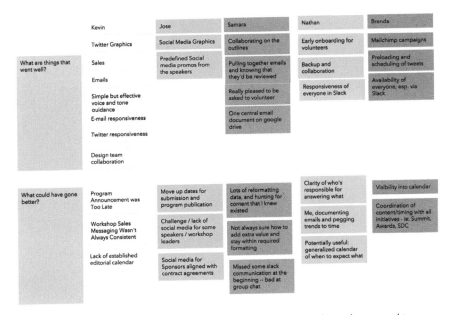

What are things that went well?

Kevin:
- Twitter Graphics
- Sales
- Emails
- Simple but effective voice and tone guidance
- E-mail responsiveness
- Twitter responsiveness
- Design team collaboration

Jose:
- Social Media Graphics
- Predefined Social media promos from the speakers

Samara:
- Collaborating on the outlines
- Pulling together emails and knowing that they'd be reviewed
- Really pleased to be asked to volunteer
- One central email document on google drive

Nathan:
- Early onboarding for volunteers
- Backup and collaboration
- Responsiveness of everyone in Slack

Brenda:
- Mailchimp campaigns
- Preloading and scheduling of tweets
- Availability of everyone, esp. via Slack

What could have gone better?

Kevin:
- Program Announcement was Too Late
- Workshop Sales Messaging Wasn't Always Consistent
- Lack of established editorial calendar

Jose:
- Move up dates for submission and program publication
- Challenge / lack of social media for some speakers / workshop leaders
- Social media for Sponsors aligned with contract agreements

Samara:
- Lots of reformatting data, and hunting for content that I knew existed
- Not always sure how to add extra value and stay within required formatting
- Missed some slack communication at the beginning -- bad at group chat

Nathan:
- Clarity of who's responsible for answering what
- Me, documenting emails and pegging trends to time
- Potentially useful: generalized calendar of when to expect what

Brenda:
- Visibility into calendar
- Coordination of content/timing with all initiatives - ie: Summit, Awards, SDC

FIGURE 9.2 This is a postmortem result that shows a decent balance between things that went well and things that didn't.

SAMPLE AGENDA FOR POSTMORTEM MEETING (1 TO 2 HOURS)

Prepare a whiteboard or wall space with each person's name along the bottom, horizontally. At the lower-right corner, leave some space with another label, called *team* or *department name* (see Figure 9.3).

DONNA   KEN   BOB   TEAM

FIGURE 9.3 Start with a blank chart before the postmortem.

CONTINUES ➤

CONTINUED ➤

List the Best Things (10 to 15 minutes)

Working together, create a list of everyone's favorite aspect of the project. Don't probe for "why" it was their favorite thing (yet). Ask each person to think about what they enjoyed about the work, and have them pick their favorite aspect. Capture each one of these above a horizon line, which lies halfway vertically on the board (see Figure 9.4).

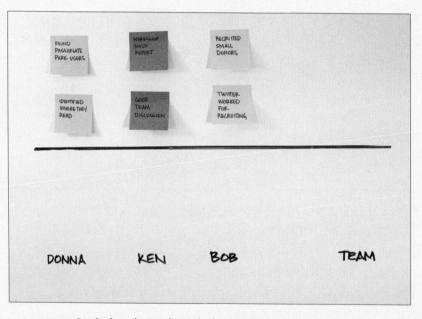

FIGURE 9.4 Put the best things above the horizon line.

Discuss the Best Things (15 to 30 minutes)

Go through each item on the list and invite everyone to reflect on why each of these aspects of the project worked well. Get multiple perspectives beyond the original contributor's. You may find that while some people perceived something as good, others perceived it as a challenge.

For example, while a project manager might see a project finishing early as a way of saving costs, a developer might have felt rushed. These paradoxes are valuable to identify and explore, so don't shy away from productive conflict. They build empathy across the team for each other's approaches. When you do identify a project positive that someone else sees as a project negative, put that below the horizon line above the latter person's name (see Figure 9.5).

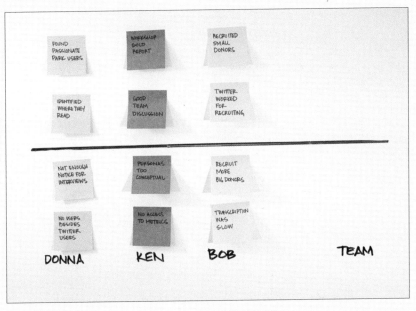

FIGURE 9.5 Begin noting negatives below the horizon line as they come up.

What Could Have Been Better? (15 to 30 minutes)

This is when some finger-pointing might take place. If it helps, consider making this discussion "blameless" by encouraging people to describe the process, and not the person, that led to a problem. As each problematic process or outcome is identified, add it to the list below the horizon line above the corresponding name (see Figure 9.6).

CONTINUES ➤

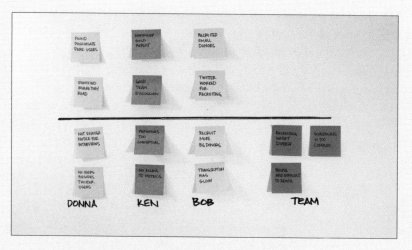

FIGURE 9.6 A completed project postmortem demonstrates a balanced discussion. Note the additional problems below the horizon line.

Capturing Actionable Insights (20 to 45 minutes)

Spend your time at the end of the meeting reviewing each column. Going around the table, ask each person what they could do differently to address the items in their negative column, beneath the horizon line. Each person can capture their changes on their own, or you can capture them publicly. Once you've finished your project with a productive postmortem, you should celebrate with an unproductive, but awesome, party!

In retros, postmortems, and other end meetings, you're going to run into some of the natural conflicts that you run into in middle meetings. Ending conflict can feel more intense, however, because a person's job, or identity, might be on the line. When that happens, you might find nonviolent communication, also known as NVC, a useful tool for managing an end conversation. Ben Sauer explains how he learned about NVC and how it has changed his approach to facilitation.

MANAGING INTENSE CONFLICT WITH NON-VIOLENT COMMUNICATION

Ben Sauer
UX Designer and Strategist, Clearleft Ltd

Ben Sauer is a senior designer at Clearleft Ltd in Brighton, UK, and a former director of The Escape Committee. He makes digital things that make sense to people and helps organizations get better at making things people need.

I was once hired to participate in a strategic retreat to develop a new vision for an old organization. The stakes were high. No one really knew where the company was going, and we were trying to bash together something coherent in three days. During the second day, one of the senior staff named Eric became visibly upset and left the group without saying much.

I was confused and disappointed. I started to wonder how this person was feeling—what he was needing or wanting—without imposing any of my own analysis of his behavior. I supposed he was feeling exasperated, impatient, and disappointed; he probably wanted to be heard, and for the group to make faster progress. I gave him a few moments to collect himself. I then approached him and asked in a very neutral tone, "You seem really frustrated. I'm wondering what it is that you're wanting from us?"

He was relieved that someone had empathized with him. He shared that he was unhappy with the progress we had made and wanted to know if we could try a different approach. We listened first, discussed some new approaches, and he rejoined the group for the rest of the retreat.

Imagine typical judgments you would make when someone gets so angry that they leave the room. What if you spoke those judgments aloud— would that help? If you don't speak them, does having those judgments in your mind affect your ability to work well with another party?

CONTINUES ➤

CONTINUED ➤

It's not uncommon to blame yourself or blame others when conflict happens in meetings. In the immortal words of Admiral Akbar: it's a trap! Moving past blame allows you to make peace, meet needs, or have difficult conversations that if avoided, end up adding more serious, standing conflict to the working relationship. Nonviolent communication helps keep you out of the trap.

What Is Nonviolent Communication?

Most of us never learn formal methods for dealing with conflict. Nonviolent communication (NVC) is a formal methodology intended to produce a shared, deeper understanding without the mess of the blame game. It's used in peace negotiations. You may think "my communication isn't violent;" the creator, Marshall Rosenberg, admitted that NVC wasn't a great title for the concept! I personally came across NVC after I got some negative feedback from a client. We were locked in battle over the direction of a product, and I started to wonder why I was having trouble connecting with people in moments of disagreement. Shouldn't we be able to respectfully disagree, but understand each other's point-of-view?

Rosenberg also wondered what blocks us from hearing one another. His answers form both a philosophy for relating to others and practical techniques for communicating in conflict. In short, Rosenberg said: "What others do may be the stimulus of our feelings, but never the cause."

You probably know someone who embodies this already—someone who remains calm and understanding and isn't triggered, no matter how others behave. Unlike other communication techniques, its implicit goal is not to fix or persuade; its only intent is to facilitate understanding. You don't need all the participants to know the technique, either. NVC can help even if you're the only one who uses it.

How Do You Practice Nonviolent Communication?

There are two basic skills in using NVC: expressing yourself and hearing others.

Expressing yourself is intended to help the other person understand you without them hearing any blame. Let's say you find yourself in a simple workplace conflict: someone has drunk the decaffeinated coffee you brewed. The four components of expressing yourself under NVC are:

- **Observations without judgments:**

  "When I see you drinking my decaf" would be better than "When you steal the coffee."

- **Feelings without attribution:**

  "I'm frustrated" is better than "You're annoying me deliberately."

- **Express universal human needs:**

  "I'd like some consideration" is more appropriate than "That is *my* coffee to consume."

- **Make a clear, positive request, not a negative demand.**

  "Could you ask me when you want some?" is more productive than "You cannot have it."

Hearing others is similar in structure, but there are no prescribed rules in forming dialogue. Hearing is intended to enable you to check in with the other party (or parties). There's usually visible relief from them when you truly connect with them where they reside, emotionally and practically. For example, "When you saw me drink the coffee, were you angry? Would you prefer for me to ask?"

CONTINUES ➤

CONTINUED ➤

Learning to practice NVC can be hard at first because it requires you to be more vulnerable than you may be used to being. It can feel a bit clunky when you try the examples provided by formal NVC, but with practice you'll find yourself using it more naturally. Consider keeping it to yourself that you're trying NVC, unless other parties in the dialogue ask why you are approaching the conversation differently. With some practice, I've found that the payoff for NVC is worth it. I have started to habitually identify feelings and needs in conversations. It's like seeing the world in a new and complex way, and it has affected all of my relationships for the better.

For more information, check out *Nonviolent Communication* by Marshall Rosenberg.[2]

2. Marshall B. Rosenberg PhD, *Nonviolent Communication: A Language of Life*, 3rd ed. (PuddleDancer Press, 2015).

WHAT YOU NEED TO KNOW

- Meetings at the end of the process can make people feel critical of one another. To make those meetings feel less like a lot of finger-pointing, balance a reflection on both positive and negative outcomes.

- When discussing negative outcomes, focus on the process, not the people.

- Identifying a negative outcome isn't enough. Be sure to facilitate past the sequence of events to identify what could be done differently in the future.

In Closing

Your time is valuable. Thank you for devoting that valuable time toward improving your meetings by reading this book. Using these ideas to explore how people spend time together will help you identify gaps in conceptual alignment, zero in on the proper level of conversational detail, and move away from aspirational behaviors toward deliberate choices to get meetings to do the work you want them to do.

Organizational self-awareness about meetings, as well as the appropriate behavioral changes needed to improve those meetings, doesn't normally spread like a virus, however. Change can be slow; in larger organizations, even glacial. You may feel disenfranchised by your meetings, your team, and your company. It's OK to feel that way, but don't let yourself get stuck in those feelings. Turn those feelings into questions, strategically asked before the meeting gets off track. If things aren't working, trigger that slow evolution toward better collaboration.

Teach your organization to design better meetings by being an active architect in the bad ones. Productive approaches in less-than-ideal situations are the most powerful long-term insurance against bad meetings that you can buy.

Index

facilitators

    for check-ins, 170

    common mistakes made by, 66–67

    in critique, 180

    designation of, 69–70

    job description, 66

    personal style of. *See* facilitation styles

Facilitator's Guide to Participatory Decision-Making (Kaner), 72

failure, learning from, 118–119

fallback script, 89

fats, healthy, 31, 38

fear

    of change and innovative thinking, 76–79

    and orienting people to change, 116

feasibility. *See* priority and feasibility matrix

feelings, questions on, 84, 87

five, groups of, 48–51

Foer, Joshua, 32

food for brain fuel, 28, 29–31, 38

G

Gamestorming (Gray, S. Brown, and Macanufo), 97, 148, 184

golden tickets, 160–161

Google, time limits on speakers, 12

Gothelf, Jeff, ix–xi, 156

graphic gameplan, 93

Gray, Dave, 97, 148, 159, 184

group member, and facilitation mistakes, 67–69

group memory, and public recorder, 68, 70

groups, breaking into, 55–56, 60

groups of five, 48–51

Grove Consultants International, The, 91, 93, 94

H

habits, 14

Hane, Carrie, 5

hippos (HIghest Paid Person's Opinion), 41

Hitch, Graham, 21

How to Make Meetings Work (Doyle & Strauss), 66, 67

humble inquiry, 83–84, 102

hypothesis design exercise, 156–157

I

ideas

    as core element of agenda building, 42

    divergent and convergent thinking, 73

    in groups of five, 48–51

    just-complex-enough concepts in a meeting, 43

    movement among people in groups, 52–56

    scaling over time, 47–48

identification of problem. *See* problem definition

imposter syndrome, 28

improvement assessments, 12–13

improvisational facilitation, 88–90

project kickoff workshops, 150–161

    goal of, 150–151

    measuring outcome of, 151–153

    sample agenda, 152–161

    time and expense of workshops, 148–149

project management software, 137

proteins, healthy, 31, 38

proud inquiry, 83, 86

public recorder. *See* recorder of meeting

Q

question design in facilitation, 86–87

questions, categories of, 83–87, 102

    that surface actions, 85

    that surface feelings, 84

    that surface motivations, 85

    that surface systems, 86

quickoff meetings, 134–137

    goal of, 134

    measuring outcome of, 135

    sample agenda, 135–137

R

RACI matrix, 152–153, 186

recorder of meeting

    recording remote meetings, 70

    role of, in facilitation, 67–68, 80

recording interviews, permission for, 133

recurring team meetings

    apply design thinking to, 7–8

    making small changes, 12–13

reflection in meetings, 27–28

remote meetings, and facilitation, 70–71

resources, framing a problem in OKR meeting, 144

responsible people, in ARCI matrix, 152

responsive web design, 115–117

retreats, organizational, 164

retrospectives. *See* agile style retrospectives

risks in project, identification in quickoff meeting, 134

Roam, Dan, 96

Roberts, Amy Mae, 36

Rosenberg, Marshall, 204, 206

Rutter, Kate, 53, 93, 94–96

S

sales meetings, 126–130

    balance between genuineness and success, 129–131

    goal of, 126–127

    measuring outcome of, 127

    sample agenda, 127–128

Sauer, Ben, 202, 203–206

Schein, Edgar, 83–84, 102

screen design critique, 180–181

scribe of meeting, 33–34

    compared to public recorder, 67–68

scripted facilitation, 88–90

scrum master, 168–169

scrums, 164. *See also* agile style daily scrum

Seiden, Josh, 156

seven plus or minus two, magical number, 47

transcription, as brain process, 22–25

translation, as brain process, 22–25

Trello project management software, 137

Tufte, Edward, 50

U

U.S. Department of Education, 149

U.S. government, Office of Personnel project, 103–104

U.S. Holocaust Memorial Museum meeting, 53, 55–56

usability testing, meetings as, 105–107

user acceptance testing (UAT) defect log reviews, 190–194

goal of, 191

measuring outcome of, 191–193

sample agenda, 192–194

V

value appropriate behavior, 108–109

visual facilitation, 34, 38, 90–97

visualization

as brain input mode, 32–34

in brainstorming session, 140–141

in critiques, 181

in lean coffee check-in, 173

in OKR meeting, 143, 145–146

in postmortems, 199–202

in project kickoff workshop, 151, 154–156, 158, 159, 161

in quickoff meeting, 136–137

revolutionary way of working, 113

in scrum meeting, 166, 169

in UAT defect log review, 192

visuospatial sketchpad, 36

W–Z

wall diagrams, 11

Walter, Aarron, 111

web design, responsive, 115–117

webcams for remote meetings, 71

weekly project check-ins, 169–171, 188

goal of, 169–170

measuring outcome of, 170

sample agenda, 171

Welch, Jack, 101

What's the Use of Lectures (Bligh), 27

whiteboarding ideas, 33

whiteboards for remote meetings, 71

"why" chain, 146–147

work-in-progress limits (WIP limits), 167, 168

working backward, 182–184

working memory, 20–22, 38

combining listening and seeing, 21–22

models of, 21, 36

scaling ideas over time, 48

workout meetings, 101

workshops, 184–187. *See also* project kickoff workshops

design of, 184

goal of, 185

measuring outcome of, 185

sample design template, 186–187

time and expense of, 148–149

Acknowledgments

This book exists because I have been fortunate enough to be surrounded by a community of smart people who want to make the world a better place.

Angela Colter served as a development editor on this book. Her empathetic perspectives, honest appraisals, and intolerance of mediocrity were crucial to its completion. She is also married to me, as of this writing. Thank you for these things.

Jess Ivins, Mike Monteiro, and Dan Brown each provided invaluable insight as technical reviewers whose expertise far exceeds my own. Thank you for your valuable time and your more valuable brilliance.

Lou Rosenfeld, Marta Justak, and the whole team at Rosenfeld Media were wonderful to work with and made me a better writer and a better person by sharing their time early and often. Thank you.

Robert Jolly, Dan Mall, G. Jason Head, Donna Lichaw, Giles Colborne, Ahava Leibtag, Dave Gray, Jeff Gothelf, Steve Portigal, James Macanufo, Jared Spool, Dana Chisnell, Jeffrey Zeldman, Karen McGrane, Derek Featherstone, Sara Wachter-Boettcher, Chris Cashdollar, Andy Budd, and Josh Clark have been priceless by saying just the right thing at the right time over a drink or a friendly meal. Thank you. The next one's on me.

Several amazing people made contributions to this book. I couldn't include everything they gave me, but if you have a chance to talk to Aarron Walter, Aaron Irizarry, Aaron Parkening, Adam Connor, Alison Beattie, Ben Sauer, Carrie Hane, Cennydd Bowles, David Sleight, Elise Keith, Ellen de Vries, Ethan Marcotte, Ida Aalen, James Box,

Jessie Taggert, Jim Kalbach, Kate Rutter, Leslie Jensen Inman, Margot Bloomstein, Megan Casey, Samantha Soma, or Sarah B. Nelson, you will be a much smarter person after the conversation. I wish I could be any one of you when I grow up.

I've worked with stunningly talented people and clients over the past two decades at companies including Capital One, Seven Heads Design, Boardthing, SuperFriendly, Happy Cog, MICA, the University of Baltimore, Goucher College, and the Enoch Pratt Free Library. Thank you for collectively building a path to this book.

To all the organizers of the many events at which I've spoken around the world, thank you for trusting me to help make your audience's lives better.

Giants have written books on this topic. I hope I've spent time adding some modest detail at the edges of the long shadows that they cast. Michael Doyle, David Strauss, Sam Kaner, Sunni Brown, and David Sibbet: thank you for your inspiration.

My mother and father were also inspiring people in their dedication to their respective careers and to our family, and I dearly miss their counsel and friendship. I'm grateful that my brother and extended family are around to remind me of what my parents taught me: what it means to work hard, work smart, and have a reason for the choices that you make.

Finally, thank you to my amazing son Owen. You inspire me every day. The time we spend together as a family learning and laughing is the reason behind all the choices that I make.

About the Author

KEVIN M. HOFFMAN connects people, ideas, and solutions in order to solve our industry's pressing design challenges. As Vice President for Design Practices at Capital One, he takes responsibility for assessing, exploring, and accelerating all areas of design with a team of more than 70 very talented human beings. Prior to working at Capital One, he founded and led Seven Heads Design, a network of digital design thinkers who collaborated frequently on major projects. Trusted by major brands over his career such as Capital One, Zappos, Harvard University, Nintendo, and MTV, Kevin's roles as design thinker, agency founder, and product manager have given him a unique perspective on how people interact when they make things. Kevin regularly shares his insights at conferences around the world.